Psychoaerobics

An Experiential Method to Empower Therapist Excellence

by Jeffrey K. Zeig

The Milton H. Erickson Foundation Press
Phoenix, Arizona

Library of Congress Cataloging-in-Publication Data

Psychoaerobics: An experiential method to empower therapist excellence / Zeig, Jeffrey

p. cm.

Includes bibliographic references
ISBN 978-1-932248-70-8 (alk. paper)
1. Hypnotism—Therapeutic 2. Psychotherapy 3. Consciousness
I. II. Title

Published by

THE MILTON H. ERICKSON FOUNDATION PRESS
2632 East Thomas Road, Suite 200
Phoenix, AZ 85016
Manufactured in the United States of America

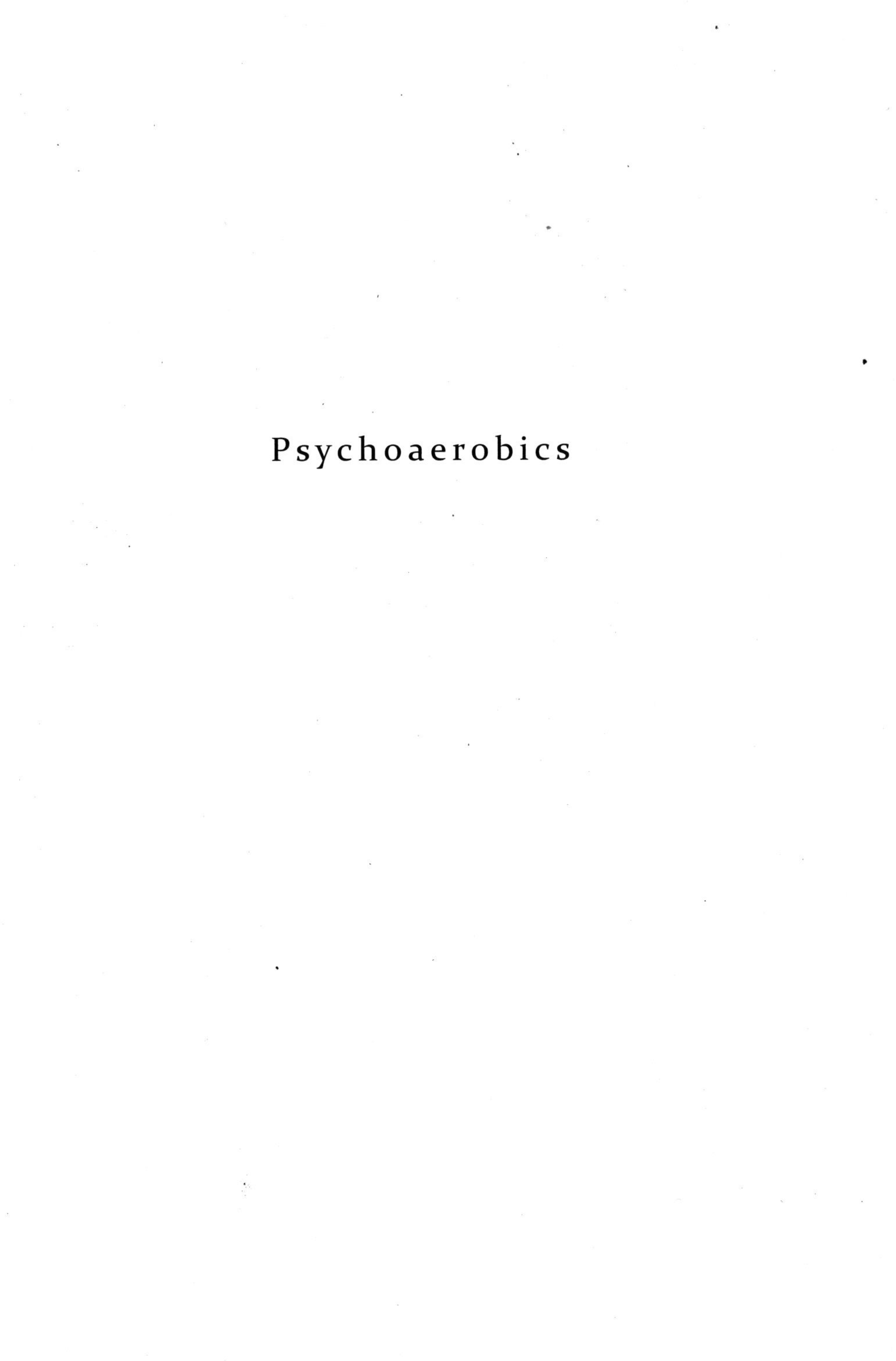

Psychoaerobics

For Nicole Zeig,
who has tutored me experientially.
Love, Dad.

Contents

PREFACE

In my college and graduate education, I was required to assimilate and regurgitate innumerable bits of information. I do not recall much of that information. What I do remember are concepts—concepts that underlie my work as a clinical psychologist, among them, empathy, transference, therapeutic alliance, and attachment. These concepts were fused in my mind through engaging experiences. But formative experiences were not the intentional design of my teachers for whom factual information was central. I look back and wonder how much more there might have been if enlivening experiences had been a cornerstone teaching method.

I remember one class in which experience was central. The professor brought in a theoretical paper authored by a psychoanalyst about why people choose to become therapists: to exert power, to love, to be a martyr, to be a voyeur, or to be a saint. The author inferred that all of the stated reasons were indicators of repressed pathology. But our professor's intention was experiential, not didactic. For weeks, each class member was required to role-play our personal reason and exaggerate the role. This exercise was my introduction to experiential training methods and how they stimulate personal growth. It whetted my appetite for embodied learning.

I vividly recall a classmate, Jane, who played a voyeur so convincingly that her "patients" had to be repeatedly switched because none of us could tolerate her voyeuristic assault. And yet, by virtue of the exaggerated process, Jane was graced with an opportunity for personal realization. Her epiphany was palpable. Sometimes when exaggerating a chosen role, a student's behavior would unexpectedly flip. John, whose reason for being a therapist was to love, suddenly became noticeably hostile. The professor's exercise was designed to prompt experiential learning—to *realize* what shaped our desires to be therapists, and how those motives could be adaptive or maladaptive. Now, decades later, my experience of that exercise remains memorably vibrant.

Okay. Let's return to the present. Having spent more than 40 years on the frontlines of mental health practice and education, I remain avid about the core concepts that have become loadstars by virtue of experiential realization. I invite you to journey with me and explore experiential methods.

First take a moment to map your customary goals when treating patients. Does your plan parallel your graduate education? Is it to impart facts? To teach theories? To endlessly explain? Do your clients need facts, theories, and explanations, or do they need generative concepts?

What about communicating with family, friends, and coworkers? When do they benefit from facts, theories, and explanations? Communicating that triad is simple and straightforward; in juxtaposition is the world of eliciting conceptual realizations. When concepts need to be realized, what is the royal road to communicating them?

Consider the world of concepts. What defines a concept? What is a fact? Facts are objective pieces of data; they are concrete singularities. It is a fact that you are reading these words. Understanding them is a concept. A concept is an abstraction: an idea of something formed by mentally combining its characteristics. Facts are objective entities; they are "left hemisphere" and conscious. Concepts live in the subjective universe; they are constructs of convenience, a synergistic amalgamation of elements. Concepts are syndromes, similar to the way in which fibromyalgia or Ménière's are syndromes, not discrete diseases. Concepts are amorphous generalizations with heuristic potential as simplifying assumptions and organizing principles.

One knows a fact; one has a "felt sense" of a concept. In the language of Martin Buber, facts are I-It. Concepts are I-Thou. Concepts are realized by empowering events. Concepts are described in generalities; they are "right hemisphere" and amorphous. Openness, conscientiousness, extraversion, agreeableness, and neuroticism are concepts. So are hope, assertiveness, protectiveness, and self-awareness. Apathy, indolence, insecurity, and worthlessness are concepts, too. Some concepts are adaptive; some are maladaptive. It is the job of the therapist to strengthen positive concepts and modify ineffective, negative concepts. Clinicians also need methods to help clients realize adaptive concepts.

There is the world of facts and the world of concepts. There is the world of space and time, and there is the world of personal experience. Science explains and organizes facts; art explores and enlivens concepts. Facts change the way we compute things, and minimizes the need for estimation. Conceptual realization alters the way we experience things. Facts elucidate the objective, external world; realizations accessorize the subjective, internal world. *Facts inform; art impacts*. Assaying the chemical composition of paint can be relegated to science. Experiencing a breathless moment when standing in front of a Picasso is the function of art. Inviting wonder is the sphere of art; explaining it is the task of science. Art is ambiguous, which is necessary to elicit and stimulate into play the intended effect. Art is evocative, not informative. If art is turned into information, the experiential effect is diminished.

Similarly, therapy is a situation of ambiguity that orients patients to conceptualize and realize, "Life can be different." The consultation room is the theater of the conceptual. Therapy is the applied art of evocative impact. In many ways, it defies science.

The sciences can be viewed as a layered progression. Physics is the foundation. From physics comes chemistry, then biology. The social sciences follow. Similarly, there can be structure for realizing concepts. Concepts are initiated from an amalgamation of associations consisting of elements that include thoughts, feelings, memories, perceptions, sensations, actions, attitudes, contexts, habits, and relationship patterns. Just as energy is required to crystalize water to ice at zero degrees Centigrade, concepts are crystallized by reference experiences, experiential shifts that are moments of emotional impact. These shifts are compounded in the crucible of an important relationship or in an empowering context. Concepts are the building blocks of "states," and "states" crystalize into identities. "I know ethical principles," is a fact. "I can be ethical," is a concept. "I am being ethical," is a "state." "I am an ethical person," is an identity. (There are additional transition points that can be facilitative, e.g., "I will be ethical," is a commitment. "I want to be ethical," is a motivation.)

There are four central propositions for this book: One, concepts, "states," and identities are assimilated experientially; they have to be lived. Two, therapists can access generative "states" that will advance their professional development. Three, therapist "states" fertilize adaptive patient "states." And four, the "states" a therapist inhabits are the territory from which interventions can be conceived.

I was mentored by Milton Erickson who was a master of eliciting "states." In interpersonal situations, Dr. Erickson communicated concepts experientially and eschewed facts. Facts can be learned from books; "states" are elicited experientially. Responsibility, creativity, engagement, connection, or presence cannot be taught didactically. Humor is the product of experiencing a joke; it is not a result of didactic instruction.

Motivation is a "state." It is stimulated into play through experiential means. There must be a phenomenological shift that is catalyzed by a significant emotional experience. It is not possible to instruct a person to be motivated though an algorithm because motivation is an amorphous "state," and algorithms are used when the outcome is a concrete entity. The communication strategy to elicit motivation resembles art, not science.

Communication can be informational or conceptual. Facts and concepts are discrete entities that are accessed through bifurcated channels: There is one channel for factual education, and another for eliciting concepts and concomitant "states."

Conceptual communication is part of our evolutionary social/biological heritage. Protolanguage used by hominids was conceptual, not factual. Vertebrates and invertebrates communicate conceptually. Concepts reach areas of the brain that were formed early in phylogenetic history; they reach primitive sides of the brain, the hypothesized focus of maladaptive psychological patterns. Problems are lodged in limbic areas of the brain, the emotional/social center. If problems were located in the prefrontal cortex, the reasoning center, they would be easy to resolve. An instruction manual would suffice. In contradistinction, conceptual communication must be lived, so that adaptive "states" and identities can be realized. We sculpt our brain according to our lived experiences.

Welcome to the worlds of conceptual communication and experiential learning,

—Jeffrey K. Zeig, Ph.D.

NOTES:

- This book is composed of four sections: Fundamental Perspectives, Warm-up Exercises, Psychoaerobic Exercises, and Concluding Remarks. The Fundamental Perspectives section consists of six introductory chapters that precede the two sections of experiential exercises. Those chapters provide the cognitive understructure that may facilitate realizations when practicing the exercises to follow. The Warm-up and Psychoaerobic Exercises are designed to galvanize the intricacies of therapeutic communication—to empower concepts and "states" that generate enduring change.
- Reading *Hypnotic Induction* (Zeig, 2014) is helpful, but not required as a precursor to this book. This book was originally conceived as the fourth volume in a series that began with *Hypnotic Induction*. The second and third books will cover advanced induction and brief therapy.
- Videos of exercises will be posted as they become available. Please see www.psychoaerobics.org for information and links.
- Readers: Please email suggestions for additional exercises.
- Facilitators: These exercises are evocative—make the environment safe.
- Researchers: Please validate any of the ideas contained herein.

CHAPTER ONE

Introducing Psychoaerobics

"If words are to enter men's minds and bear fruit, they must be the right words shaped cunningly to pass men's defenses and explode silently and effectually within their minds."

—J.B. Phillips (writer and clergyman, 1906-1982)

What people *know* and what people *realize*; what can be understood, and what can be conceptualized are islands unto themselves. Although the gulf between them should be easy to traverse, this isn't always so. We know to be kind in our relationships, we know to establish good habits, and we know that we can alter our moods, but, do we *realize* what we know? We have to "get" these concepts, and establish concomitant "states." To paraphrase Voltaire, the heart has a mind that the head doesn't understand. It can be challenging to bridge the distance from the head to the heart.

What is the heartland of psychotherapy? And how can clinicians help clients discover it? Clinicians want clients to realize what they know. Contemporary practice is based on psycho-education. Sometimes, psycho -education is the slow road. Sometimes, it's the wrong road. Realization requires something experiential, a more distinct shift in "state" than knowing something intellectually.

Simply stated: *The experiences one lives are a bridge between the land of the knowing and the land of realization.* It is not "book learning" that affects changes in "states," it is lived experiences.

Didactic education is central to many fields, especially the sciences and mathematics. But some things must be learned experientially. Happiness is one of them, because happiness is an emotion. Similarly, becoming motivated, being aware, feeling successful, or having faith must be realized experientially because they are concepts and "states." Emotions, concepts, and "states" are realized as experiential shifts; they cannot be taught in the same way that mathematics can be taught. One does not memorize the equation for happiness.

Emotions, moods, and "states" are distinct. Emotions are fleeting, visceral, adaptive experiences that are directional. They are generated automatically based on the history of the organism. Fish, reptiles, birds, and mammals experience emotions. Emotions regulate activation and response, both internally and socially; they are attempts to promote adaptation. Emotions are social magnets that automatically attract or repel. Emotions prompt animals to move toward or move away. Evolutionary design is such that even one-celled organisms move toward or move away, and that may be the precursor of emotional signals. Perhaps on the phylogenetic scale, tropisms in plants are even more elementary precursors.

Moods can be considered calcified emotions. A person can be stuck in an angry mood or caught up in an elated mood. Moods have duration, but they may not serve as an adaptive function in one's growth and development.

"States" are different. Psychologists would not categorize motivation, presence, awareness, faith, meditation, responsibility, or openness as emotions or moods. Many human experiences are best categorized as "states." I initially put "states" in quotation marks because they are difficult to define, being a temporally variable amalgamation of emotions, moods, relationship patterns, physiological arousal, psychological habits, and contextual determinants, to name a few. (For more information on "states," see Zeig, 2014.)

I am liberal in my exploration and definition of states for heuristic value. Loosely defining states helps students actualize the goal postures that are the central topic of this book. But, leniency has its price. I sacrifice precision to promote effectiveness. And, effectiveness is central to psychotherapy. In some situations—especially in emotional relationships—being effective trumps being right.

People seek help when they are lost in inflexible states, feeling unable to summon resources to generate effective states. Limiting states, such as feeling victimized, can be replaced with generative states of empowerment. After all, it is axiomatic that *whoever has access to the widest variety of states is most likely to determine an adaptive outcome in any given situation.* With the widest assortment of states from which to respond, chances are a person will find one that could be effective. This axiom applies to clinicians and patients, parents and children, and business managers and employees.

Again, states (and emotions, moods, and identities) cannot be promoted through didactic means. If someone lacks motivation, pointing this out will not motivate that person. Motivation (and other states) must be elicited experientially.

Experiential communication is the purview of art. Film, for example, is a "show don't tell" medium. Film, fiction, poetry, painting, theater, dance, music, fashion, interior design, and architecture are uniquely capable of eliciting alterations in mood, perception, concept, and state. So, how is art taught? It cannot be taught with didactic methods; the shift to the state of creating art and becoming an artist must be realized experientially.

Artists use conceptual communication that diffuses information in favor of ambiguity. Art is interpretive; it is subjective, phenomenological, and interactive. Methods used universally by artists are designed to elicit, not inform. Art is created to evocatively stimulate an experiential shift. Science, on the other hand, is objective. It is the opposite of phenomenology, which is the study of lived experience.

Art and science are reciprocal. Heisenberg's uncertainty principle states that if you know information about the momentum of a particle, you sacrifice information about location. Clarity and emotional impact can be reciprocal. Science extols clarity; art extols experiential impact.

Art is the exploration of emotions, concepts, and states; all art centers on emotional impact. Art is a human necessity because it exercises emotions, concepts, states, and identities, and it keeps them supple. If therapists envision eliciting constructive emotions, concepts, and states as essential, they should look to art for models, because art stimulates realizations.

Filmmaking is the most complex art, and it is highly valued across cultures. Moviegoers don't actually want to be hunted by a dinosaur or risk life and limb in a high-speed car chase, but they may enjoy experiencing the fantasy. My most recent project involves studying the structure of filmmaking in order to understand how movies elicit emotional response. I now teach therapists (and others) how to use those methods to impact states and emotions.

Emotions are social currency. We trade them. We bank them. We invest in them. Emotions engage us in the world. To have impact, artists sculpt emotions, musicians sculpt time, attorneys sculpt justice. A therapist sculpts concepts. Therapists use emotional experiences as the combustion engine that propels adaptive momentum. Therapy is about experiential empowerment.

Human communication is best conceived as an art, not a science, especially when it is designed to have emotional impact. To develop my skills as a psychotherapist, I work diligently to improve the art of communicating in a way that empowers people. Hence, I study art and I also study the work of master clinicians who are artists at interpersonal impact.

In more than 40 years of practice as a licensed therapist, I have been privileged to personally know many of the masters who advanced psychotherapy during the latter half of the 20th century and the beginning of the 21st century. As communication artists, however, they were eclipsed by my mentor, the esteemed psychiatrist, Milton H. Erickson, MD (1901-1980). It is not hyperbole to say that he was the world's greatest psychotherapeutic communicator. His skill in helping patients and students to access adaptive states is legendary. He mastered conceptual therapeutic communication; rarely was he didactic in the consulting room. Even his teaching was conceptual, designed to elicit states.

For example, I listened to lectures that he conducted in the 1950s and 1960s when his audience was primarily physicians. The lectures seemed like extended hypnotic inductions. When I asked him about this, he explained, "I did not teach content. I taught to motivate." I was stunned. It took time to comprehend the meaning of his reply. I had no experience with someone who taught to elicit a state. My previous teachers focused on content. Erickson seemed to extol form over content. Form trumps content when it comes to eliciting states. What was Dr. Erickson's design? When he was offering therapy, providing hypnosis, or even teaching, his goal was to help people realize adaptive concepts and states.

In 1973, I became Dr. Erickson's student, and for the next five years I traveled frequently to Phoenix to learn from him. In 1978, I moved to Phoenix to be closer to him. Beginning in 1977, I conducted workshops on Ericksonian methods. I have taught Ericksonian practices in more than 40 countries. Primarily, my focus has been training psychotherapists, but I also offer programs for other professionals, including attorneys, dentists, and life coaches. Additionally, I present lectures for the public. My initial teaching style was didactic. I explained theories and techniques. Gradually my teaching mirrored Erickson's orientation. As I evolve, I am becoming increasingly experiential—a closer approximation to Dr. Erickson's approach.

Dr. Erickson was the most radically experiential teacher I ever encountered. He minimized didactic information, which, after all, can be learned by reading. He used hypnosis, stories, metaphors, tasks, games, jokes, and fragments of poetry and literature to elicit conceptual realizations. Subsequently, I searched for models that would help both me and my students better emulate the masterful results Dr. Erickson achieved. The best models came from art. My earliest investigations were with improvisation.

My sister, Sande Zeig, is an artist who has expertise in filmography, directing, writing, and acting. During a conversation many years ago, I commented to her that offering psychotherapy is closer to the art of improvisation than it is to science – and that I wanted to know how actors learned improvisation. "Take a course," she advised. Because I am a leader at following directions, I enrolled in three successive adult education courses in improvisation. The defining experiences I had in the improvisation lasses prompted me to develop the Psychoaerobic system.

Psychoaerobics is an experiential model for helping clinicians *be* better therapists through systematic, experiential learning. The premise is that clinicians (and people in general) who strategically develop constructive states will be more effective, independent of their explicit theoretical orientation. Psychoaerobic methods can also be modified to embellish clinical practice and supervision. There is applicability to any profession or any life endeavor when the goal is to help the recipient of the communication alter state and perception. Psychoaerobics, moreover, is a method of modeling.

Modeling is a method of improving excellence that can be realized in five steps. One, find someone who is excellent at her craft. Two, study her closely, Three, divide her states and concepts into a series of manageable units. Four, decide which units are personally fitting. Five, practice those units experientially until you improve your excellence.

The Psychoaerobic Exercises that you will encounter are especially designed for psychotherapists. Many of the exercises model methods that are used to train actors. When I began to study improvisation, I looked for books containing improvisation exercises. The work of Viola Spolin, as well as that of Keith Johnstone, was pivotal.

In improvisation training, there are warm-up exercises that precede more complex acting exercises. In the Psychoaerobic system, there are warm-up exercises that model the generic excellence of a good therapist. The Psychoaerobic Exercises that follow, model the excellence of Milton Erickson and the states he most frequently inhabited.

The experiential process can be harnessed to elicit concepts and "states" that can help professionals *be* better clinicians. Eliciting concepts and states, moreover, can promote personal development in any occupation. The Psychoaerobic system presented in this book is based on structured, experiential exercises that are systematically organized around discrete conceptual domains. The emphasis is on experiential methods of personal realization; the exercises are *not* meant to teach specific techniques or particular skills, though these may be learned along the way.

Domain-specific training can happen outside the therapy room. A series of conceptual domains are identified in the Psychoaerobic Exercises. The exercises foster realization of those domains. Repeated practice is required. Practice, practice, practice, until realization is seamless.

Once the domains have been developed outside the therapy room, they can be used in therapy and in life. They can easily transition from working memory to automatically being activated in procedural memory. Personal preference will dictate the domains that a given reader might want to develop. Choose the domains that are of special interest. The exercises in this book do not need to be practiced sequentially in order to be effective.

Many of the exercises focus on hypnosis, an area in which I specialize, but it is not necessary to have a background in hypnosis. Studying hypnosis has been instrumental in my own development as a clinician. Although I intermittently use formal hypnosis in my practice, I almost always use concepts from hypnosis to empower the therapeutic moment. Studying hypnosis prompts clinicians to strengthen their message—to make it more beautiful. Hypnosis is a way of making a message more aesthetically pleasing, and thereby more effective. Hypnosis teaches therapists a technology of altering states. Hence, I recommend that all clinicians learn hypnosis, even if they don't use it as a primary orientation.

The exercises you will encounter are designed for groups, but many can be modified for individual practice. The Psychoaerobic system can be used in therapy training programs, and it can be used in clinical supervision. The system is a metaphor for experiential training. It can be modified for any profession, and for any relationship, when the target is to elicit concepts and states.

When the goal is to have emotional impact, when the goal is to promote conceptual realizations, when the goal is to alter states, experiential methods are pivotal. The best prescription is often an experience (rather than medication).

This is a book about improving excellence. I will assume that readers are excellent. Therefore, the focus is on using experiential modalities to expand on existent excellence and promote mastery. Mastery flourishes in the domain of conceptual realizations. The essential units in this book, therefore, are concepts, not facts.

SECTION I
Fundamental Perspectives

"We learn through experience and experiencing,
and no one teaches us anything."

—Viola Spolin,
Improvisation for the Theater

CHAPTER TWO

Psychoaerobics: A Playshop Approach for the Development of the Therapist

Unlike most works in the field of psychotherapy this is not a book about theory, research, or psychotherapeutic methods. In fact, this is not a book at all. It is instead a manual of exercises designed to elicit from clinicians new ways of empowering themselves and their patients.

Psychoaerobics is an innovative method for teaching personal development states. It is a system for honing personal excellence in professional and nonprofessional settings. The fulcrum of change is experiential empowerment.

Although the primary exercises in this manual are based on principles developed by Milton Erickson, the template can be used for modeling experts in other fields, such as music, athletics, and teaching. The model can also be used to improve parenting. The underlying orientation is simple: Facts can be taught didactically; concepts are garnered experientially.

This manual consists of 60 experiential exercises (plus numerous variations) focused on specific domains of therapist development. Psychotherapists can use the exercises to become more effective communicators. The exercises can be modified for patients to create powerful therapeutic experiences. They can also be used for experiential supervision. Attorneys, life coaches, teachers, and others can alter the exercises to promote personal excellence. Nonprofessionals can use them to build an experiential repertoire for personal success. The purpose of the exercises is to improve interpersonal communication whenever the goal is conceptual or emotional.

Communication is a skill that can be studied didactically, but fundamentally it is learned experientially when one is a child. In graduate school, psychotherapy, a highly sophisticated form of communication, is primarily taught didactically as a conglomeration of theories, rules, techniques, and research studies. Students of psychotherapy become technicians who learn to apply rote procedures, including how to do systematic desensitization, how to offer proper interpretations, how to do EMDR, and myriad other formulaic methods of therapist/patient communication. Yet, when students actually begin to work with patients, they soon see that something else happens. Linear theoretical rules just don't stay simple and tidy.

Let me take you on a little excursion that will illustrate what I mean, and illuminate why the current approach to teaching psychotherapy (and other concepts, states, and identities) would benefit from a shift in emphasis.

Imagine that you wake up tomorrow possessed by an uncontrollable desire to become a patient in psychotherapy. Of course, you wouldn't be ready-made for psychotherapy. You would have to prepare yourself. How would you go about doing this? Quite simply, you would begin by orienting yourself to one, or any combination of the following domains: *I can't...; I never...; I always...; I should...; If only...; What if...?; Maybe...; and If he/she/they would only...*

You might begin by recursively communicating to yourself: "I *can't stop* overeating." Or, "I *never* have any satisfactory relationships." Alternatively, you could suggest to yourself, "I'm *always*_late." Or, "I *should* read more books." Reaching for grand, global assessments from the past, you could pummel yourself with, "*If only* I had chosen differently in life." You could beam into the unpredictable future: "*What if tomorrow during my flight the plane has a mid-air collision?*" Or, you could add uncertainty and self-doubt into the mix: "*Maybe* it would be better if I did 'X.'" *Maybe* it wouldn't. *Maybe, maybe, maybe.* (One can make a case for almost anything that follows a "maybe.") And, don't forget to lay blame elsewhere: "*If only he/she/they would* be more sensitive, be kinder, be more affectionate, be more responsible, be more reasonable," etc.

Diligently employ some combination of these orientations with great frequency and verve and you will quickly create limiting concepts and states. Continue, and you will transform yourself into a prime candidate for psychotherapy. Practice the ineffective state frequently, and you can adopt an ineffective identity, e.g., "I am a failure."

Now, psychotherapists, hold for a moment this image of a self-created patient entering your office while you settle comfortably into your professional chair. Your job as therapist is to undo the patient's sense of victimization —a victim of feelings, thoughts, behaviors, attitudes, history, and/or relationships. You must devise a way to change the patient's "I can't," the orientation of victimization, into a concept of "I can," the domain of empowerment. "I can cope effectively." "I can do things differently." "I can change."

But, effective psychotherapy is not merely a matter of helping clients change their thoughts or vocabulary. Patients exist in ineffective states. Their vocabulary may be an indicator of the state they are in, and perhaps the identity they have adopted; it is not a cause of the state or identity. Now, let's turn to the therapist.

The process of becoming a therapist is not predictable and circumscribed. You cannot say one or a combination of things to become a therapist. To be effective, therapists cannot adopt one concept, state, or identity. Many schools of psychotherapy have formulated a set of rules, delineating what is essential for treating a client. But, all schools share an underlying purpose—helping clients transform from victims to victors. Regardless of the theory and methods to which a therapist subscribes, effectiveness can be improved by developing constructive therapist states. Moreover, therapists' states can be a starting point for inventing effective treatment.

I can illustrate with an incident from my personal experience. In 1985, the Evolution of Psychotherapy Conference brought together the world's reigning experts in psychotherapy to celebrate the 100th birthday of psychotherapy. (Some historians trace the birth of psychotherapy to 1885 when Freud first became interested in the psychological aspects of medicine.) As the organizer of the Evolution Conference, I had the privilege of listening to the lectures of many remarkable theorists and practitioners.

I attended a presentation by Joseph Wolpe, the pioneer behavior therapist, who spoke about treating depression. I listened avidly as he described the necessity to discover the patient's underlying anxiety, to schedule the anxiety-provoking situations by severity, and then to carefully and methodically desensitize the anxiety from least to most stressful. After I heard this, I thought, "No wonder I'm having difficulties with my depressed patients. I'm not using the technique of scheduling and desensitizing underlying anxiety."

Mulling this over, I wandered down the hall, certain I had found a clue to offering better therapy. But, something nagged at me. "It must be more," I thought. "Surely, therapy must *more than* identifying and desensitizing underlying anxiety."

In another room, the great psychodynamic psychotherapist, James Masterson, expounded, "If you have a borderline patient, use confrontation. It's the proper medicine. For a narcissistic patient, use empathic mirroring of narcissistic vulnerability. It's the proper medicine. If you use empathic mirroring on the borderline, it won't work. Confrontation will not work for the narcissist." "Aha," I thought. "No wonder I'm having trouble with my borderline and narcissistic patients. I'm not using the right medicine."

"And yet," I pondered, my thoughts becoming more crystallized, "therapy with borderlines is more than confrontation; with narcissists it's more than empathic mirroring."

Next, I wandered into the room where the humanistic therapist, Carl Rogers, illuminated the understructure of the patient's feelings with empathy, genuineness, and positive regard. "Yes," I thought, "be more empathic. That's the ticket!" Yet in another room, Salvador Minuchin advised, "Don't look at the individual. Look at the structure of the relationship between people. Modify the structure of the relationship and people change." "Minuchin is right," I told myself, "I need to study systemic methods of family therapy."

And yet...

All of these presenters seemed intrinsically right about their perspectives. Their theories and methods seemed eminently sound, and each had specific rules about how to approach psychotherapy. However, specific advice about how to *be* a psychotherapist was sparse.

By the end of the Conference, I was awash in practical and theoretical contradictions. What I ultimately learned was that I differed from Wolpe, and Masterson, and Rogers, and Minuchin in that I had a lack of theoretical certainty. Project *their* kind of certainty into a therapeutic situation, and it may not matter what your entry point is —be it behaviors, attitudes, feelings, cognitions, or relationships. As a clinician, when you have a state of certainty, the patient responds, perhaps more to the certainty than the intervention itself.

As an inspiring clinician, I say with a touch of irony, find some concept, be it theory or technique you believe in, present it back to your clients with conviction, and patients tend to conform and change. In this sense, psychotherapy is akin to a religious conversion. The state of therapeutic certainty provides clinicians with the courage obtained from their fantasies, which is twice as good as the courage from their convictions.

I don't have theoretical or absolute technical certainty. My convictions are different. I believe therapy is more than —more than confrontation, more than changing people's attitudes, and more than manipulating interpersonal structures. *Therapy should be a symbolic, experiential drama of change, the implicit imperative of which is, "By living this evocative experience, empowerment will result."* Therapy happens by virtue of establishing and blending adaptive concepts and concomitant states. Changing thoughts, behaviors, feelings, and relationships is valuable but less central, unless those changes are in service of eliciting effective concepts and states. To create constructive experiences, focus on states in both the client and clinician—states that are experientially elicited through conceptual communication.

Yes, there is a strong experiential tradition in psychodynamic methods, dating at least to Franz Alexander and the corrective emotional experience, but in psychodynamic methods, change is a result of understanding. But, experiences should be the main course. Understanding can be the entrée or the dessert. *Dynamic experiences can precede psychodynamic understandings, both in providing treatment and in improving therapist excellence.*

Due to other experiences I had at the 1985 Evolution Conference, my professional confidence rallied. I attended three additional presentations that resonated powerfully with my underlying predilections: lectures by R.D. Laing, Carl Whitaker, and Virginia Satir. These extraordinary presenters improvised; they weren't based in science, theoretical rules, or research. Their models of influence stemmed from philosophy, literature, and theater. Throughout the course of civilization it has been art in all its forms and guises that has had the greatest power to influence people to grow intrapsychically and interpersonally. It is art that creates emotional impact. It is art that modifies perceptions, concepts, and states.

In response to my discovery, I revamped my orientation toward therapy. I came to see therapy as an art rather than a science. As a result, I was forced to reconsider my approach to teaching psychotherapy. Over the years, I spent a considerable amount time learning and teaching technique. Yet, as I looked back at the development of psychotherapy as a discipline, I realized that the emphasis on technique is a recent phenomenon. Therapy started with a focus on the personal development of the therapist.

Historical Reflections in Training

It is a curiosity—perhaps with an Oedipal imprint – to reflect on the nature of how professionals have been trained to be therapists.

In psychotherapy's early days, there wasn't much to learn regarding technique. Inquiry focused on theoretical issues. When Freud investigated the psychological aspects of medicine, he first studied hypnosis. Then, he rejected hypnosis in favor of his method of free association. Freud delved into why people were the way they were. He built elegant theories. His method emphasized understanding history, thereby ridding patients of the templates from the past that confound the present. He called these templates "transference." A primary goal of psychoanalysis was to free the patient of transference, the projection of historical conflicts and patterns that impeded adaptive living. Psychoanalysis would guide the patient to understand problematic transference projections. To foster transference, Freud used the couch, creating the anxiety-provoking situation of free association. The patient was expected to say whatever came to mind. The shadowy analyst would sit out of sight, which also created tension. Hence, the arrangement in the consultation room was ideal for evoking transference in the patient so that it could be analyzed and understood. Change would happen as a correlate of understanding. The techniques of practice were rather simple, consisting of confrontation, clarification, and interpretation.

Psychoanalysts were physicians. The training of psychoanalysts focused on the development of the therapist. The purpose was to develop the analysand as a tool of therapy. Psychoanalysts were to evolve into a countertransference-free state. Physicians who had elected to become psychoanalysts, spent years undergoing a training analysis, learning to rid themselves of their own distortions and transferences.

A consequence of Freud's method was that the therapist state was designed to be relatively invariant. The analyst would assiduously avoid any countertransference (unhelpful projections of the analyst's historical conflicts). Shifts in the analyst's state could be considered countertransference, which would confound patient transference.

After World War II, there was a proliferation of divergent schools of psychotherapy. Europe was in shambles and the locus of therapy moved to the United States. Attention focused on practical methods and theories that could have wide applicability. The development of the therapist receded into the background. Eventually, procedures became "medicalized" and algorithmic. (The implication in medicine is that a happy surgeon is as effective as an unhappy surgeon, both of whom know the proper technique.) As techniques proliferated, the state of the psychotherapist in offering procedures seemingly became unimportant, perhaps subsumed under what is called in research studies, "nonspecific factors."

A more encompassing approach doesn't educate clients to change, but invites them in a compelling way, much as an artist invites a shift in perspective. When therapy is conceived as an art rather than a science, clinicians can reinvent themselves as communication artists. Subsequently, methods of learning therapy must be revised. To learn physics, attend a scholarly lecture. But one cannot learn how to create art or succeed as an athlete in the lecture hall. Rather, learning can proceed from the inside out, by discovering and honing concepts and states within.

Historically, the development of the therapist was central to pristine psychoanalysis. Let's return to that concept, but with a significant twist. The development of the therapist (communicator) once again becomes a central axis for promoting effective results, but with more depth and flexibility. Similar to psychoanalysis, it can be the starting place for treatment.

Consider the current models for teaching therapy. Are they effective for training therapists? If not, what would be a better model? What about study acting, and, more specifically, improvisation? How do artists learn their skill?

Whenever we interact with another person we are improvising. In the psychotherapy office, the same holds true. Interestingly, not only did many great clinicians start with hypnosis, but many had backgrounds in drama. Fritz Perls, Peggy Papp, Jacob Moreno, and Virginia Satir had experience in acting, which they put to use in the craft of influence as teachers and therapists.

Following my sister's advice, I signed up for some theater lessons to learn how improvisation is taught. I joined several 20-year-olds in weekly classes. Our instructor, who had a Ph.D. in drama, began the initial session by asking us to introduce ourselves and state our goals for the class. The first student, John, exclaimed, "I'm here because I want to do theater." Next, Jane: "I'm here because I want to do movies." Next, Jim: "I'm here because I want to do commercials." Then, Jeff: "I'm a spy. I want to learn how a dramatist teaches improvisation."

After the introductions, we all stood in a circle for our first acting lesson, a warm-up exercise called "la-las." The task was to repeat a vocal pattern —la-la-la-la-la-la-la!; la-la-la-la-la-la-la!; la-la-la, la-la-la; la-la-la; la-la-la; la-la-la-la-la-la-la!—while adding a bodily motion, in this case, handclapping.

At first, the teacher led the exercise and we were to copy what she did. After a while, she told me, "You will be the leader. Pick a different consonant. Use the same rhythm. Pick a different motion." So I chose, pa-pa-pa-pa-pa-pa-pa, and made a cradling gesture. Everyone copied me. The next student selected ga-ga-ga-ga-ga-ga-ga and a new movement. The teacher then stepped outside the circle to offer feedback. "No, Jeff," she said, "Not ga-ga. *GA-GA!* Listen to the leader, use her emphasis and watch her. Copy her sweeping movements." When the exercise was over, we simply went on to the next exercise. No discussion. No processing of what just happened. No analysis. No connecting the dots.

I entered a state of confusion. "Wait a second," I protested. "Aren't we going to talk about this? Share the meaning of this experience and discuss it?" "No," she replied, "next exercise." By nature I'm a shredder.

Give me something and I will dissect it, separating the wheat from the chaff. Patients tell me their issues; I can dissect the conundrum to discover useful essentials. They tell me their histories; I dissect them. They describe relationship problems; I dissect them. I reduce their story to essential units and feedback components. I am skilled at this regurgitation process —chewing up the patient's story, digesting it, and returning it in a more palatable form.

But when the acting teacher refused to dissect our experience, suddenly I had palpable uncertainty, similar to the feelings I had during my consultations with Dr. Erickson. He would toss something out to me in the form of hypnosis—a task, an allusion, a riddle, a game, or a diagram—which would propel me into an experiential moment. I would wobble with uncertainty, but inevitably my instability would lead me to stumble forward. I was supported by Dr. Erickson's attentive care. I knew he would right me if I started to fall. The force of the intentional uncertainty was balanced with the force of intentional care. The uncertainty was surgery. The care was anesthetic. And, there is no surgery without anesthetic.

Commonly, Dr. Erickson would not discuss the meaning of his offering. Instead, I would activate to "unpack" the experience and discover personal meaning. It was like visiting an art museum where it's up to the viewer of the art to unearth realizations.

In the improvisation class, we were lumping; we were not shredding. Suddenly, I activated. I wondered, "What is this about? What am I learning? What skills are being taught? What states and concepts are necessary to do drama?" One necessary skill is articulation. To perform on stage, an actor must have good articulation. I recalled the teacher's observation, "No, Jeff. Not ga-ga. *GA-GA!*" I was prodded to learn articulation, but as a concept, not a skill.

A stage actor does not shy away from big gestures; such movements create impact. As a psychotherapist, this element was most foreign to me. I had learned to sit still when I worked, restraining my body as much as possible. Now, I was being asked to use gestures (and intonations, postures, and movements) strategically for effect. That lesson alone changed my orientation to therapy. Strategic intent comes first. Embellished interventions can be targeted to a specific outcome. I began to use my body (and as many communication channels as I could muster) to effect goals.

The final concept I gleaned from this one improvisation exercise was the importance of modeling. To act, you must model. If you are going to become a character, a taxi driver, let's say, you better observe taxi drivers and model their behavior. If you need to be in character as a homeless person, then you better find some and observe their behavior.

I concluded from this simple warm-up exercise that these three concepts—articulation, large gestures, and modeling—are important in acting, but this lesson was never stated. The teacher did not begin class with a lecture about the first three rules of acting: articulation, big gestures, and modeling. Instead, we engaged in an exercise. The realization and conceptualization of articulation, big gestures, and modeling would be garnered implicitly. They would become states that we would enter while on stage; they would not be techniques. It was as if we were circumnavigating the left hemisphere. We were establishing states that would bypass working memory and more immediately become procedural memory. We use working memory to learn a skill by deliberate practice. Eventually the skill becomes automatic. At first, the mechanics of swinging a tennis racket takes effort, but after a short while it becomes second nature.

Implicit procedural learning is valuable in mastering certain motor skills or cognitive abilities. It is how children learn language. Implicit procedural learning must be experiential. Compared to rote memorization, it conserves time and energy.

The method used in the acting class was not the kind of learning I was exposed to in graduate school. It was more on par with taking a bicycle out for the first time, straddling the seat, putting a death grip on the handlebars, and pushing off.

Learning to ride a bike is a visceral experience based on implicit procedural learning. You don't learn it in your left hemisphere. And memorizing the physics of riding a bike doesn't help you stay balanced and glide through space. You learn to ride in your body. To grasp the concept of momentum, you have to be on the bike trying to keep your balance, developing an implicit awareness of all the ways your body movement affects direction and stability. You try it once, you fall, and you try again. After a while, you are doing it. Your body learns, and you've *got it*.

Remember the breathless, "Aha!" feeling when you learned to balance on a bike? Psychotherapy and training psychotherapists should be based on eliciting a wonderful "Aha!" in patients and students that evokes generative change. The "Aha!" moment is when one grasps the concept.

Milton Erickson did therapy that way. Dr. Erickson was a dramatist first, a scientist second. This may sound peculiar because Erickson spent the first 20-plus years of his career as a researcher. But Dr. Erickson's research was more like an anthropologist's than a laboratory scientist's. He did field studies rather than empirical research.

When Dr. Erickson offered therapy, it was drama. His interactions with patients came alive. Perls, Whitaker, Moreno, Minuchin, and Satir had similar approaches. They incorporated drama into their therapy because they were interested in direct encounter, not the mere transmission of didactic information. All of these experts made drama central when training clinicians.

To my knowledge, Dr. Erickson never studied acting, but his teaching methods were comparable to those used in training actors. He avoided didactic lecturing. He taught by using experiential lessons — lessons the recipient invariably had to activate to unearth personal realizations.

The Psychoaerobics system creates an environment for therapist development, based on learning that is experiential and implicit so that change quickly becomes procedural. Similar to the experience of building and strengthening muscles in aerobic training, the Psychoaerobic approach mandates practice.

To better understand the place of therapist development in clinical practice, a Metamodel of therapeutic communication is outlined in Chapter Three.

CHAPTER THREE

Choice Points: The Metamodel

To understand the Psychoaerobic method in the context of clinical work, a larger Metamodel about communication is presented. The model consists of five intervention Choice Points: *goals*, *gift-wrapping*, *tailoring*, *processing*, and *the position of the clinician/communicator*. The model is a template that will strengthen emotional impact, and it can be applied in any interpersonal situation.

I use experiential exercises in teaching students each of the five components, in order to help them master concepts. In order to teach the position of the communicator, I rely on experiential exercises in the Psychoaerobic system.

The Choice Point Model is illustrated in Figure 1:

Let's briefly examine the first four aspects of the model, and then address the fifth component in its unique role as an axis, around which the other four revolve. Each Choice Point has a primary question.

A Choice Point that can be considered first is the *goal*. The goal question is, "What do I want to communicate?" Reformulated, the question could be, "What is the response I hope to elicit?" Seemingly, a goal should be easy to formulate, but many times, and in many situations, specific outcomes are not intentionally clarified by speakers prior to communication. People often speak to understand their own thinking, and they may not think strategically about the effect they want to achieve.

In medicine, goals are algorithmic. For example, if a patient has a certain type of infection, 10 different physicians make the diagnosis and prescribe an antibiotic. There is a clear decision tree. However, psychotherapy is driven by heuristic processes—simplifying assumptions based on past experience. Therefore, 10 therapists may have 10 different goals/

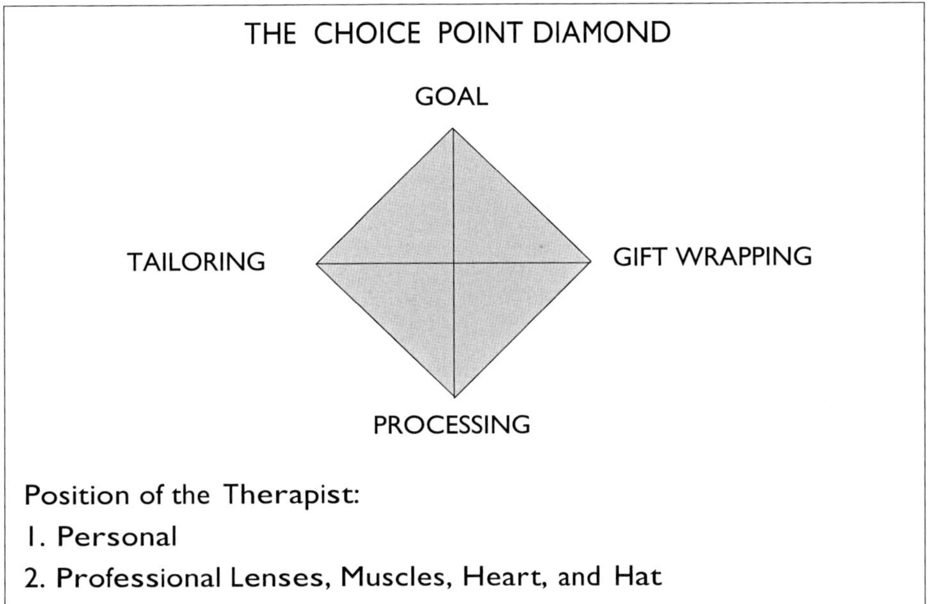

Figure 1

procedures for the same condition. One clinician may suggest changing thoughts, while another recommends altering behavior. One may prescribe emotional understanding, while another offers relationship counseling. Goals vary for many reasons, one of which is the theoretical predilection of the clinician.

Gift-wrapping is the second component. The gift-wrapping question is, "How do I want to communicate the goal?" It is important to know what to say; it is imperative to decide how to empower it. The didactic component for therapists concerning gift-wrapping is extensive. It consists of information on applying techniques, including hypnosis, the use of anecdotes, symptom prescription, and reframing. In medicine, a nostrum may cure a malady. It is erroneous to think that a psychotherapy method works similarly. *Techniques of therapy are ways of presenting gift-wrapped ideas to patients; they are not curative in and of themselves.* Proper gift-wrapping enhances effectiveness, especially when the goal is emotional impact. Metaphor is one way of gift-wrapping a message.

Aristotle said, "The greatest thing by far is to be a master of metaphor." Presenting a goal within a metaphor can enhance responsiveness.

Metaphors activate a search for personal meaning. They shape one's psychic landscape and communicate the unknowable; the representation and object disappear as the fences of formality and opposition dissolve. Metaphor is conceptual communication that activates a dormant representation and fosters emotional impact in order to elicit realizations. Metaphors stimulate concepts; they are not vehicles for presenting facts.

Gift-wrapping within a metaphor enhances impact. A metaphor is indirect. When Romeo says, "Juliet is the sun," we realize what he means. Impact would have been lost if he explained in detail. The metaphor is more than the words, but it is ambiguous. Interpretation can vary from person to person, but conceptual meaning is universal, as in the case of Romeo's proclamation.

The third component, *tailoring*, is an essential way of strengthening a message. To tailor a message the therapist/communicator asks herself, "What position does the patient/receiver take?" This component focuses on assessment of the patient's intrapsychic and interpersonal life. The information garnered is used to modify the gift-wrapping to fit the individual. Tailoring is also used for establishing goals.

Interventions should be gift-wrapped to fit the uniqueness of an individual. Presenting an assignment to a scientific person requires one approach. A different tactic is needed for an artistic person. The scientist might be given a logical, linear rationale for the task. For the artist, the task might be framed as a desirable image.

Understanding the position of the client may be instrumental in determining the goal. If a client complains about depression, map how the individual expresses it. For some, it will consist of being internally preoccupied and socially withdrawn. For others, dark images and negative recriminations predominate. For many, central facets could be anhedonia and ennui. Goals may emanate from the map of how the person experiences the problem. The route to follow may be indicated by the structure of the individual's orientation to the stated problem. *The principle for social interventions is to treat components, not categories*. The stated problem is a category. When enough components have been altered, the category will change.

The fourth component is *process*, and the pertinent question is, "How can a dramatic process enliven the gift-wrapped and tailored goal?"

There are three stages: the setup, intervention, and follow-through. The process is: enter, offer, and exit—what one does before, during, and after. Consider the stroke of tennis or golf. The power comes from the setup and follow-through. In movie language, the process is clean entrance, presentation, and clean exit. For example, there can be an establishing shot of a building, followed by a dialogue between two people in an office, and then music or voices segue into the next scene.

Good communicators, who want to have emotional impact, make their message into a tripartite process. For example: 1.) "You are reading this book." 2.) "You can understand the ideas." 3.) "You can realize the concepts." 4.) "And you can use those understandings with intent to empower your communication with emotional impact." 5.) "Because you want to be more effective, do you not?" In this example three "pacing statements" (1, 2, and 3) lead to the goal directive (4), which is sandwiched between the pacing statements and the motivating rationale (5). The tripartite process used in this example is: pace, suggest, and motivate.

Attending to four intervention points empowers interventions. One of the merits of this model of intervention is its immediate utility: The clinician has more choices when encountering resistance. As needed, one can change the goal, gift-wrapping, tailoring, or process.

Again, the first four components can be taught both didactically and experientially. Experiential methods are preferred because they promote procedural learning. Guided exercises can be used to effect realizations. The first four Choice Points answer a larger question: *How does one DO therapy?*

The last Choice Point, the position of the communicator, can be primary in improving outcomes. This Choice Points speaks to the question: *How can one BE a therapist?* To increase impact for the receiver, the communicator can access previously dormant states. The Psychoaerobic method can promote communicator flexibly and elicit states (postures) that help to achieve targeted impact.

The Posture/State of the Communicator

To investigate the communicator's posture or state, consider the question, "What position/state/posture should I take?" The state of the communicator can be divided into four subcategories: lenses, muscles, heart, and hat. Each of these elements has both a professional and personal aspect. Lenses represent ways of viewing. On a professional level, lenses acquired when studying family therapy diverge from those learned in behavior therapy. On a personal level, the lenses acquired growing up in one's family of origin differ from those learned in a neighbor's family. Muscles are the way of doing. Psychoanalysts, for example, hypertrophy their interpretation muscles, whereas Ericksonians develop their storytelling abilities. Compassion is manifested according to one's heart and varies according to both therapeutic approach and personal orientation. And finally, the hat symbolizes the communicator's social roles. "She wears many hats" refers to having several social roles. Being an artist is a social role. So is being an athlete, or being a parent, or being a confident professional. The hat of a psychoanalyst is not the hat of an Ericksonian.

Figure 1 illustrates the model. Note that the posture of the communicator is central. It impacts the other four Choice Points and those Choice Points are interactive. The starting point does not need to be the goal. Some therapists have decided the technique (gift-wrapping) prior to talking to the client. They can be so adept and convinced of its effectiveness, that therapeutic change ensues. Some clinicians emphasize specific goals and contract for agreed upon changes. Other therapists may not specify goals, and consider therapy to happen by virtue of an "I-Thou" relationship. Existential therapy, for example, deemphasizes goals, techniques, and strategic processes, and centers treatment on building the immediate interpersonal relationship in the consulting room. Sometimes it is best to take time and start with tailoring to understand the position (values) of the client before deciding the goals.

In order to communicate with impact, all five Choice Points should be considered. The state of the therapist/communicator, the central aspect of this book, is further developed in Chapter Four.

CHAPTER FOUR

The Posture (State) of the Therapist

Let's consider in-depth the fifth Choice Point: the posture of the therapist. I will use the designation "therapist," but those from other fields can substitute "communicator." Each therapist brings to the consulting room personal and professional postures that, to a large extent, determine the outcome and course of treatment. As far as techniques are concerned, personal positions may be especially influential. Erickson's ingenious interventions were commonly derived from his state, not from theory, research, or practice.

The personal position or state of the therapist is an admixture of the therapist's orientations and values. At any given moment, each therapist projects an essential posture in the consulting room. The course of therapy may spring from these headwaters.

Again, in classical psychoanalysis, the professional position of the clinician was invariant in order to foster transference. In psychoanalytic schools, the personal position of the therapist could be considered "countertransference," a term that is laden with negative connotations because the therapist is to assiduously avoid projection of residual, personal, unconscious conflicts into the therapy situation.

Therapists project their values onto patients, as well as their expectations about the course of therapy, through their demeanor, dress, office policies, and consulting room design. Maladaptive projections must be avoided, but one cannot help but project, just as one cannot avoid manipulation. The goal is to construct and utilize therapeutically helpful projections. Of course, according to classical psychoanalysis, projection is always negative.

In all schools of therapy, each clinician has a proscribed orientation consisting of specific "lenses" (input operations), "muscles" (output operations), "heart" (compassion), and "hat" (social role). These components are central in helping the patient construct a more adaptive and fulfilling existence. The acquisition of lenses, muscles, heart, and hat are formed by the overt or implicit exigencies of specialized training and experience. The orientations become set within a range, representing the technical posture or state of the therapist.

Shaped by professional training, components of the clinician's technical position are activated. Some therapists focus on behavior, others on feelings, and others on relational patterns. Some intervene with caring tones, others with humor or stories. Some are formal. Some are casual. A therapist's lenses, muscles, heart, and hat are an idiosyncratic blend of natural abilities and acquired characteristics.

In the field of psychotherapy, there are widely differing opinions on the composition of the "correct" lenses, muscles, heart, and hat a therapist must have. There is no one answer to the question: "How can I be the most effective therapist?" The individuality of each patient makes it impossible for a single therapist posture to be correct for everyone. Moreover, the quarks or essential elements in one school of therapy are quirks in another (Zeig, 1987). In this sense alone, therapy is best conceived of as an art, not a science.

In science there is generally agreement on fundamental components and their definitions. In psychotherapy, no such agreement exists. Are fundamental units of psychotherapy behaviors or feelings? Id or Child Ego State? Awareness or cognition? Relationship patterns or psyche? Although the essential units of specific theories are concepts, they are often treated as facts. Additionally, across schools of therapy multiple definitions exist for core concepts. In the field of hypnosis, for instance, professional organizations attempt to standardize a definition of the phenomena, but other, equally plausible, definitions exist. Clinicians cannot even agree on the purpose of treatment. Some experts insist on specific goals; others argue that therapy is a growth experience and concrete goals are antithetical to the process.

Goals in psychotherapy are not universal. In the practice of medicine a diagnosis is a treatment plan. In psychotherapy goals are determined by the interaction of the position of the client and the posture of the therapist. If the patient complains of depression, the therapist can subdivide the complaint into treatable units. Alternatively, the therapist can guide the patient to examine history, relationships, behaviors, dreams, or existential goals, all of which can lead to successful outcomes. The goal can be negotiated between client and clinician. The therapist can suggest, "You don't have depression, you have despair." The therapist alternatively suggest, "You have anger turned inward."

The lenses, muscles, heart, and hat compose the "Who am I?" of the therapist. This posture can be a starting point in treatment. It can determine the direction of treatment and its outcome, as much, and sometimes more than the position of the patient.

For a simple illustration of the power of the posture/state of the communicator, consider the following anecdote, which is perhaps apocryphal.

A female cousin of Queen Victoria had dinner on subsequent nights with two great British statesmen, Gladstone and Disraeli. When asked about her experience she explained, "The first night was dinner with Gladstone. At the end of the dinner I was certain that I was with the most intelligent man in all of England. The second dinner was with Disraeli, after which I was certain that I was the most intelligent woman in all of England." Independent of the content of the conversation, the posture/state of the communicator probably accounted for the evoked sentiment.

Certain postures are endemic to all therapists, regardless of their theoretical orientation. Competent therapists demonstrate empathy, genuineness, and positive regard for their patients. Therapists cannot let personal needs and problems interfere with a patient's treatment. Effective clinicians strive to create a therapeutic alliance.

It is understood that in successful therapy the therapeutic alliance accounts for much of the variance. An alliance is a concept and a state. Trying to train students to form an alliance didactically is taking the slow road. Experiential methods are needed to flexibly access therapeutic alliances that are case-specific.

A therapeutic alliance is not just a coordination of goals within an empathic context; it is an amalgamation of domains, many of which depend on the flexible states the therapist inhabits. The subtext of this book is about developing states that will implicitly strengthen the therapeutic alliance.

To review: Therapists develop certain individualistic and highly specific postures and states, and many are bound to the principles advocated by their particular theory. As a follower of Erickson and a practitioner of his methods, I will present quite a different posture from that of a behaviorist or psychoanalyst.

On Therapist Evolution

Aspects of a therapist's posture continue to evolve through training and experience. Traditional professional sources of growth and development include graduate school, post-graduate training programs, supervision, studying research, and, of course, interacting with a variety of patients. Lectures, modeling by experts, reading books, using media, and conducting co-therapy are additional avenues for professional expansion. Although these are effective methods to improve one's skills, they are not particularly experiential.

Most therapists, regardless of their theoretical persuasion, would ascribe their professional evolution to some combination of the aforementioned sources. But, when querying clinicians about the primary source of their growth and development, a reflexive response, "Primarily, I have learned from my patients," is the platitude. Over time it occurred to me that this statement could have many meanings. Learned what? Learned how to be a victim? Learned how to be inflexible? Learned how to complain? Okay, I should not be such a smart aleck, but here's the point: Why should an important issue like professional growth and development be amorphous? Is a more systematic method possible? Can one conceive of therapist development as being parallel to sports training, which requires personal experience, practice, and discipline? At a certain level, once a skill set has been mastered, the athlete's focus is on being in the Ideal Performing State (IPS) to accomplish the immediate task; it is not focused on mechanics.

As communication "athletes," therapists can evolve by regular training (and cross-training). Emphasis can be placed on developing flexible therapeutic postures that could serve as situation-specific IPSs. Techniques would not predominate.

The Psychoaerobic program is meant as a start for a systematic, experiential training program.

CHAPTER FIVE

The Posture (State) of Milton Erickson

As discussed in Chapter One, the primary purpose of the Psychoaerobic system is to identify unique lenses, muscles, heart, and hats that can improve personal excellence, especially when the goal is emotional impact.

Dr. Erickson exemplifies what it means to be an effective therapeutic communicator. He developed a number of postures during his career. For example, Dr. Erickson championed the concept/state of utilization, and he developed his acuity to perceive useful details of patients' patterns. Further, Dr. Erickson used indirection, a state I call "orienting toward." He was radically experiential and created dramatic therapeutic experiences around which change could constellate. Also, he was strategic, developing therapy in intentional steps. Dr. Erickson worked to strengthen the therapeutic message by first accessing states complementary to the message, including utilization, acuity, orienting toward, being experiential and being strategic.

Yes, I know that the list of Erickson's orientations are not "states," in the strict sense of the definition, but designating them as such has heuristic value because they can form the foundation of clinical work. The Psychoaerobic system is a method to explore and develop effective states so that they can be seamlessly applied in practice.

Dr. Erickson offered countless examples of how clinicians can flexibly change states and postures. Despite years of habitual behavior, despite the intellectual arguments of our favored theoreticians, and despite our personal predilections, we can shift our position as required by circumstances and patients' needs. The exercises in this book constitute something like a good yoga workout —designed to activate new sets of muscles, allow our lenses to become sharper, pump fresh blood into our hearts, and add color and texture to our professional hats.

ERICKSON'S SELF-TRAINING

A model of the self-training of states is suggested in Dr. Erickson's work. He reported a number of exercises that he used to train himself. To compensate for omissions in his medical school, internship, and residency training, in one of his early jobs, he would get a written social history from the social work service and compose an intuited, traditional psychiatric mental status examination based on the social history. Then, he would take a mental status examination and compare the intuited one with the actual mental status examination. Subsequently, he would reverse the process: He would get a mental status examination, write an intuited social history and compare it with the actual social history from the social work service. He said that he did that exercise with a hundred patients. His attempt was not to learn content, but to master a posture, a state of realizing fundamentals of human development that would become procedural.

Erickson also worked to access a state of acuity. He attended to nuances in human social behavior. Early on in his career, working like Sherlock Holmes, he would discern a clue and venture a written prediction. To avoid self-deception, he deposited his prediction with his secretary to be placed safely in a lockbox to await confirmation. For example, perhaps he noticed telltale behaviors and ventured, "This person is having an affair." Or he would surmise, "That woman is pregnant," although physical signs were nonexistent. He worked avidly to develop a posture of extrapolating from minimal cues; he was not just focused on increasing his base of cognitive knowledge.

Throughout his life, Erickson was dedicated to his growth and development. Not long before his death, I asked him a simple administrative question. He responded by telling a story in which his answer was gift-wrapped. I had to unwrap the answer. His decision to not directly reply to my question was interesting to me. He was communicating conceptually rather than didactically. I had the sense that he was playing. Even more, he was exercising his orienting-toward state, wanting to keep it supple.

Dr. Erickson spent much of his life in a state of orienting toward. He worked to improve his ability to orient toward so that it would become a state from which he operated. For instance, one of Dr. Erickson's primary gifts as a therapist was using therapeutic stories. But storytelling was derived from a state of orienting toward; it wasn't a technique. When his children came to his office to visit him, he told them stories. Dr. Erickson often told stories to his patients. He also frequently told stories when he was at dinner with friends and family. The purpose was to stimulate into play conceptual understandings.

Dr. Erickson might tell a story to see if he could get his listener to pick up his pen, turn it around, and put it down, without ever directly asking them. This wasn't manipulation for the sake of manipulation. Dr. Erickson was exploring human responsiveness. He was the consummate social psychologist before social psychology was a recognized professional field. And, to help students develop states, he offered experiential assignments.

Erickson gave me personal development assignments, although not systematically. For example, he told me to go to a school yard and watch children. I was to predict which child would go to which toy next, who would leave the group first, and who would speak next. The substate of acuity, extrapolating from cues and inferring future patterns, was near and dear to Erickson, and he encouraged this posture in his students.

As a conceptual communicator, Erickson commonly used experiential methods. During my first visit with him in 1973, he drew three lines on a piece of paper—one vertical, one horizontal, and one diagonal. "What is this?" he inquired. I looked carefully. I tried to discern a pattern. I gave up. I had no idea. Erickson dramatically nodded, then shook his head, and then twisted it to the side, indicating simultaneously "yes, "no," and "I don't know." He was teaching me to look for minimal cues. He said I should watch clients carefully when they speak, and be aware of incongruities. The simple, but experiential nature of his approach was so indelible that it is alive within me more than 40 years later. Had he explained the need to notice incongruities solely in didactic terms, it would not have made the same impression. I would not have "gotten" the concept.

The Psychoaerobic Exercises model vital components of Dr. Erickson's orientation. Just as modeling is important to acting, modeling is also a useful tool for psychotherapists. I have chosen Dr. Erickson as a model, but I do not confine myself to Ericksonian methods. I use family therapy, transactional analysis, gestalt, systemic approaches, and psychodynamic therapy, yet I continue to be impressed with Dr. Erickson's unmatched skill in preserving his experiential orientation in psychotherapy. I work to incorporate Ericksonian states into my practice in a way that honors my personal style.

I often adopt a theme of the month, something I work to develop on a professional or personal level. For example, I might dedicate time to being more visually perceptive. I might work on developing the state of utilization or mastery of the three-step, strategic process: enter, offer, exit. My personal training method is to experientially foster in myself therapeutic states.

The Psychoaerobic method can be used for many aspects of personal development. A more complete orientation to the method is provided in the next two chapters.

CHAPTER SIX

The Psychoaerobic Orientation

The Psychoaerobic orientation centers on developing generative concepts and states. Experiential exercises are used to help students realize the felt sense of the goal state.

Before presenting the Warm-up and Psychoaerobic Exercises, a quick review: There is a basic subjectivity about offering psychotherapy that cannot be avoided. For one thing, the experiential state of the clinician is idiosyncratic. It is projected into the therapy situation and forms part of its core. Therapists with didactic postures use teaching methods, whereas charismatic practitioners have their magnetism as a therapeutic core. The posture of the therapist influences the therapy. Therapy often proceeds from the states the therapist assumes. The Psychoaerobic system is based in conceptual communication. Therapists who are conceptual will assume a unique posture because communicating concepts primarily requires an experiential orientation.

The mainstays of clinical training include didactics, supervision, research, modeling, clinical experience, books, media, co-therapy, and a one-way mirror. Training can also develop the clinician's posture/style/selfhood/orientation/ways-of-being/states, in which case a systematic, experiential program is desirable. As I have evolved as a teacher, I have added a core component to my teaching: a method to foster therapist states experientially. It is a process that I learned from Erickson, but any school of therapy can expand training to elicit and evolve core postures experientially. The intended audience for Psychoaerobics is not limited to students of Erickson's work. The Psychoaerobic system is a model that can be modified and used in many disciplines of therapy and in many aspects of life. Considered as a whole, the Psychoaerobic system as a metaphor for experiential human development: Find excellence, divide it into components, discover which states are best for you, create exercises to develop goal states, and practice those exercises until they become procedural.

There are two groups of exercises: Warm-up and Psychoaerobic. The Warm-up Exercises primarily access postures that are generic to most clinicians. They also prime orientations that will be further developed in the Psychoaerobic Exercises.

The Warm-up and Psychoaerobic Exercises are meant to be practiced repeatedly. Let's return to the analogy of learning how to ride a bike. It may have looked easy as you watched other children glide by smoothly, but it took practice in order to realize how to balance. Each time you practiced there was implicit progress, until suddenly you "got it!" What felt like a sudden learned skill was actually a cumulative process. Similarly, the exercises herein must be practiced to fully actualize the orientation for which they are designed to elicit. The result can propel clinicians into new worlds of effective therapy.

The exercises that you are about to encounter were specifically conceived for psychotherapists, and they were meant to be conducted within a training group. However, modifications can be made for use with individuals, in a graduate school classroom, in a study group, in supervision, in clinical practice, or for personal development in a non-clinical setting. The overarching purpose is to help develop effective, empowering states.

Again, I am taking license in using the word "states." I am using the concept broadly. Let's say, for example, that one state the therapist wants to develop is the use of metaphor. Strictly speaking, the use of metaphor cannot be considered a state. Rather, it is commonly considered a tool for communication. For present purposes, however, it is useful to consider it a state.

Recall Shakespeare's metaphor, "Juliet is the sun." Note that Shakespeare did not use the simile, "Juliet is like the sun." The propositional meaning of a simile would have been weaker. The metaphor he used is richer in implicit meaning, more open to interpretation, and... more apt to lead to a change in state of the actors and audience.

I cannot imagine that Shakespeare was thinking mechanically or deliberately, "Now I will create a metaphor that expresses the depth of Romeo's infatuation." As an accomplished writer, creating metaphor was procedural, an automatic experience. I imagine that Shakespeare effortlessly transitioned into a state in which metaphor would "just happen." Perhaps he lived in that state.

Metaphor is conceptual communication that elicits experiential realizations. I encourage students who attend my training programs to develop the use of metaphor to their maximum ability. To do this I devise experiential exercises to help them to shift into a state from which metaphor can flow. To create a memorable anchor, I might tab this "the Juliet is the sun" state.

One reason for positing metaphor construction as a state is that it can override the intrinsic drive to be right —to do things correctly. A metaphor is ambiguous; it is an interpretation, and there is no right metaphor. Moreover, I want the learning to evolve as quickly as possible so that it will seamlessly transition to procedural memory rather than languish in working memory. "Sacrifice being right," I advise students, "and develop the felt sense for which we are striving." Consciously limiting students' learning of intellectual content, I instruct them to develop a state, and to begin to realize the experiential parameters of that state.

Discussion after each of the following exercises should focus on the participant delivering the communication, not on the recipient. The communicator is asked to describe a phenomenological characteristic (or two) of the orientation for which the exercise is intended. The communicator strives to realize markers of entering the goal state (as best as it can be realized at that moment). Thereby, it is proposed that the goal state can be effortlessly retrieved in applicable situations.

Students often find the directive about focusing on the communicator pixilating because they are compelled to try to be effective for the recipient. They want to learn how the recipient understood the message. As much as possible I discourage that quest – and often even prohibit it. I want the communicator to self-direct, and examine the experiential shift that happens when realizing the orientation for which the exercise was designed. Effectiveness can wait; it can be a byproduct of developing the goal state. Focusing on the state rather than the response of the subject helps students develop generative, conceptual realizations.

Now let's turn to therapy and hypnosis. When patients come to therapy, they may be in a state of feeling like a failure. They may have developed an identity of being a failure. It does not help to lecture them about the steps they need to take in order to succeed. Dr. Erickson's solution was to work conceptually to elicit effective states. The underlying principle centers on dormant resources. We all have unrecognized potentials. People who identify as failures have actually succeeded in life more than they have failed. The focus of therapy can be to awaken previously dormant resource states, and that's where hypnosis comes into play.

A couple of observations about hypnosis: In common culture, hypnosis is considered to be an anesthetized state in which the operator surgically removes maladaptive patterns from the subconscious and inserts constructive ones in their place. Erickson revolutionized hypnosis, conceiving it as a procedure that would awaken people to latent strengths, both physiologically and psychologically. Moreover, Dr. Erickson used formal hypnosis only a fraction of the time. He developed a procedure he called, "naturalistic trance," which could be considered "hypnotherapy without formal trance." Hypnotic procedures can be used without a traditional induction because hypnotic methods experientially empower emotional impact. Hypnotic procedures demonstrate to patients that they can change their state.

Those who want to learn more about hypnosis can read *Hypnotic Induction* (Zeig, 2014). For present purposes, hypnosis can be considered one of many experiential procedures. Hypnosis is evocative, conceptual communication. It is not a vehicle for presenting didactic information. Other experiential methods include storytelling, tasks, symbolic assignments, paradoxical assignments, ordeals, jokes, and metaphor. All experiential methods are designed to alter concepts, states, perception, sensation, memory, emotion, identity, and calcified relationship patterns.

Therapy can be a process of eliciting "reference states" or "reference experiences" for a goal. Reference experiences can be created or elicited. If a patient presented to Erickson complaining of being a failure, he might arrange a situation in which the patient would experientially realize success. He might use methods that would appeal to, and awaken, a history of success. Alternatively, Erickson might work to elicit a state of success by telling a series of anecdotes within the therapy session that would orient toward components of being a success. Anecdotes have, as do most forms of communication, both an informative level and expressive level; there is overt content and evocative undertone. The manifest content of the anecdotes might be benign, but the latent content would orient the client to develop an experiential shift into a felt sense of being successful. Experiential methods can modify states because they are evocative communication. Changes in states must happen by virtue of realizing presented concepts.

Some reference states are buried in memory, outside of a person's immediate reach. Even if you know that a particular resource is in a library, it does not mean that it can be easily located and accessed. Every unsuccessful person has reference experiences of success, but those experiences may not have crystallized into a concept, state, or identity. Life-shaping events, such as rituals and ceremonies, are designed as reference experiences that will form identities. It does not mean that just because one gets married or divorced the person assumes the respective identity. Locked in memory are reference experiences that are positive or negative – experiences that shape identities of being intelligent, humorous, capable, or worthless and unlovable. Reference experiences that create identities are defining moments. They are elicited through experiential methods, such as storytelling.

Often, when I was with Dr. Erickson, he would tell me a series of stories. Vaguely realizing there was a unified thread that connected the stories, I would say, "I think there is a theme that runs through the series of stories that you just told me, but I cannot grasp it. What is it?" Sometimes he would tell me. Most often he would tell another story. It would not be the cognitive understanding that would help me achieve growth and development. Rather, he designed his method to create experiential shifts—changes in state that could be generative.

For example, Erickson extolled flexibility and worked to promote a "beginner's mind" in his students and patients. Flexibility was one of his universal themes. He called upon and used his encyclopedic repertoire of flexibility categories to tailor the message for the individual. He might chain together a series of stories about children, adolescents, or adults, and how they could adapt flexibility, often choosing the category to parallel the developmental level of the patient's presented problem. Or, he would tell flexibility stories about animals, or different cultures. When I met Erickson I was in my mid-20s and was somewhat rebellious. Paradoxically, he would tell me a series of stories about patients' ridiculous rigidities. I would silently chuckle to myself, "Oh, I don't have that sort of absurd rigidity." But, implicitly, I was examining my own rigidities and concomitantly developing a state (a reference experience) of being more flexible. Erickson's method was conceptual, and designed to create existential shifts. Stories were often a vehicle for his experiential orientation.

Just as cells create organs and organs foster organisms, concepts and states are chained together over time to create identities. We all have multiple identities, most of which are functional. We may be a husband, a teacher, a father, a friend, etc. Some identities, such as being a failure, are maladaptive. Shifts in states and identities are often seamless, but they can be identified. Moreover, signs of shifting states and identities can be made conscious. Focusing on components can help access states.

To clarify the idea of components, consider an emotion. Take anger as an example. What are the signs of being angry? Perhaps you thrust your jaw forward, ball your fists, tighten your stomach muscles, raise the volume of your voice, or develop a form of tunnel vision directed to the object of your ire. Curiously, even if you are in a peaceful mood, if you engage in a number of those actions, you can elicit feelings of anger.

Now think about states. How do you know that you're motivated? Present? Altruistic? Curious? Ethical? Successful? Interested? What are the shifts? Similarly, one could examine any of the myriad identities that are assumed during the course of the day and recognize central components.

The purpose of the Psychoaerobic system is to elicit goal states in the communicator. It is assumed that generative states in the therapist will facilitate effective states and responses from the patient. It may be the case that neither party cognitively understands the events that precipitate effective states. But, knowing markers could be especially useful to the communicator.

Discussion among participants after the Psychoaerobic Exercises should be directed to developing the goal state of the communicator. Each exercise is designed to elicit a specific state/orientation/identity/posture. To facilitate discussion, a number of component categories can be used to describe the goal state. I will list them in no particular order.

This template, the States Table, may be useful as participants engage in discussion at the end of the exercises.

It should be noted that many of the components in the table are output operations that can be used to elicit adaptive concepts and states by creating experiential impact. The components compose the palette of the therapist. Clinicians should be able to use any and all of them to create experiential impact that elicits in patients adaptive concepts and states. Erickson used all the "colors on his palette" to foster change. For example, tonal and gestural characteristics can be used strategically as elaborations during storytelling because they increase the density of the message, thereby making the story even more evocative.

STATES TABLE

- Behavior
- Affect
- Thought
- Attitude
- Perception (visual and auditory experience)
- Sensation (tactile experience)
- Additional senses: Olfaction, Proprioception, Gustation, and Kinesthesis
- Imagery/Fantasies
- Memories
- Relationship patterns, such as Openness and Proximity
- Relationship to the Environment
- Energy Level
- Gestures and Expressions
- Posture
- Vocabulary
- Linguistic characteristics: Prosody, Direction of Voice, Voice Tone and Tempo
- Attention and Concentration

This list is by no means comprehensive. Other categories could be used, including analogies, qualities (intensity and duration), and conspicuous absences. Examples of conspicuous absences include not using adjectives, voice tone variation, or expressive gestures. When debriefing after the exercise, it is not necessary to have a descriptive phrase for each component. But keeping the categories in mind can help participants to better characterize a shift in state.

By way of explanation, I will return to the state of motivation and present a hypothetical sentence for each of the categories. The central question is, "How do you know that you are motivated?"

The following sentence stem can be applied to the categories in the States Table. "I knew that I was motivated because..."

Behavior: I shifted my body forward.
Affect: I felt happy.
Thought: "I could accomplish the goal easily."
Attitude: I liked how I was in the moment.
Perception: I noticed visual details. I was unaware of extraneous sounds.
Sensation: I could feel my feet solidly placed on the floor.
Additional senses: I lost track of my position in space.
Imagery: There were three-dimensional patterns in my mind.
Memory: I remembered playing baseball as a child and really wanting to help the team win.
Relationship patterns: I moved closer to the person to whom I was attending.
Relationship to the environment: I was unaware of anything other than the person to whom I was speaking.
Energy level: I was full of energy.
Gesture and Expressions: My arms were open; I was smiling. My gestures were directed forward.
Posture: I was standing straighter and more upright.
Vocabulary: I was using more positive adjectives.
Linguistic characteristics: My voice was more melodic.
Attention and Concentration: I was extremely focused.

It is impossible to completely describe a state. But once the recipient can more clearly and comprehensively identify one or two characteristics of the IPS (Ideal Performing State), she can create a reference or anchor for accessing that state when needed.

For example, I saw a one-man play, "I Am My Own Wife," in which the male actor transformed himself into 30 different characters —male and female, young and old. There was a slight but perceptible, unique behavioral shift prior to enacting each role. The behavioral shift seemed to be an anchor that fostered the alteration in role.

Accessing effective states is essential for competitive athletes. During the course of my career, I have worked with professional athletes from many different sports. I query them about their IPS. The IPS for a golfer is different than the IPS for a football player, and it varies depending on circumstances. I work to help athletes establish an anchor for their goal IPS. Similarly, therapists can have an IPS. The Psychoaerobic system can help clinicians develop and access their IPS, and the concomitant concepts that precede an IPS. Eventually, the IPS becomes an identity.

Chapter Seven presents the format of the exercises to follow.

CHAPTER SEVEN

Psychoaerobics: An Introduction

Dr. Erickson was not systematic in his approach to training, but the Psychoaerobic model is designed systematically. The concept behind the Warm-up Exercises is as follows: Envision an excellent therapist, divide her states into a series of components, and devise exercises to help students realize component concepts. I created the Psychoaerobic Exercises similarly: Envision Erickson, divide his states into a series of components, and design exercises to help students realize those substates. In both instances, the process consists of modeling.

The permutations of the Psychoaerobic system are endless. The approach is a metaphor for improving excellence; for being a better person. Find an expert —parent, teacher, businessperson, artist, or athlete —then use the modeling process to create experiential exercises to access and "try on" substates.

There is an underlying teaching principle: *Create the dots, don't connect them.* Allow the patient or student to connect the dots. Connecting the dots for a patient or student can be a compulsion for clinicians and teachers. On the surface it may seem to be a good method, but if an experiential shift is the goal, it is best if the client/student connects the dots spontaneously, thereby creating generative realizations. Experiential exercises are the dots that can activate comprehension.

Allowing the receiver to connect the dots is the subtext of all art. Remember, art is conceptual, not factual. Unfortunately, expository writing often centers on connecting the dots. In the sections to follow I am going to be more didactic and descriptive than I might be in an interpersonal situation. Such is the limitation of writing a book. My hope is that the reader can surmount this obstacle by practicing the exercises with the intent of developing experiential realizations and existential shifts.

I began developing the Psychoaerobic system in the early 1990s, which was before I took a class in improvisation. One of the first exercises I created addressed the state of utilization (see Psychoaerobic Exercise 36), a central concept in Ericksonian practice. A number of Psychoaerobic Exercises are designed specifically to help students actualize a state of utilization. (For more didactic information see the chapter on utilization in my book, *Confluence*, 2006.)

As time progressed, I developed more exercises in response to my increasing interest in helping clinicians be better at their craft, and I incorporated them into my training programs. By the mid-1990s, I had created almost all the exercises that you will encounter. Thus, I have tested the exercises with hundreds of my workshop attendees. Some exercises have been revised extensively. Over the years, I have shaped these exercises into more polished forms. Even so, several are still works-in-progress. The exercises that I use most frequently in my teaching programs have the most extensive discussion sections. Those that are works-in-progress may not have discussion sections. I hope that the reader can creatively hone the less polished exercises into useful forms.

I included embryonic exercises because I want the Psychoaerobic system to be available for study and research. I want to promote the themes that therapist development can be experiential, and that therapist states can be a starting point for therapy. The guiding heuristic is simple: *Whenever the goal is to communicate with emotional impact, whenever you want to promote a conceptual realization, whenever the goal is changing a state or modifying an identity, establish an experiential moment that will empower that goal and create a reference experience.*

There are a number of different categories around which each exercise is organized. The following are primary categories:

1.) The clinician Posture orients the participant to the goal concept, or state.
2.) The Format indicates the number of participants recommended for the exercise.
3.) The Roles can be decided arbitrarily by the participants.
4.) The Method is the recommended procedure for the exercise.
5.) Many of the exercises have Variations so that they can be used for multiple purposes. Some can be incorporated into therapy or

supervision.

6.) The Purpose summarizes some of the intended experiential outcomes.

The exercises should be done slowly and methodically. Many should be done in slow motion. The purpose is to elicit experiential realizations. Work to discover a marker for identifying the goal state so that it can be anchored for future use—and so that it eventually becomes procedural. The exercises should be practiced multiple times until a "felt sense" of the goal state is realized, until there is an experiential shift. For most people, practice is necessary; these are not exercises that can be done once.

The setup for some of the exercises has to be explained by the group leader. The handout for some exercises should not be presented until the exercise has been completed, because studying the handout prior to the exercise would confound the intended effect. Keep in mind that some of the exercises might be beyond participants' comfort zone and that no one should be pressured into taking part.

To further describe my intention, discussion is provided after some of the exercises. I elaborate a bit more than I might in the course of the workshop, where I give primacy to experiential realization over didactic understanding. Again, it is my intent to feature video examples of some exercises online at www.psychoaerobics.com, and add more examples over the years.

Warm-up Exercises are presented in the next section. The single-spaced format allows for easy duplication. Teachers can freely copy exercises for students, as long as they are copied exactly as printed here.

SECTION II
Warm-up Exercises

(Recommendation: Give to participants after completing the exercise.)

"Experiencing is penetration into the environment, total organic involvement with it. This means involvement on all levels: intellectual, physical and intuitive."

—Viola Spolin, *Improvisation for the Theater*

EXPERIENTIAL EMPOWERMENT
PSYCHOAEROBIC$_{SM}$ Exercises
www.psychoaerobic.org

WARM-UP EXERCISE 1

Clinician Posture to Develop: A resource state for participating in **PSYCHOAEROBIC**$_{SM}$ Exercises—incompetence and playfulness.

Format: Dyads

Roles: One Pitcher; one Receiver. The roles switch in the second iteration.

Method: The Pitcher and Receiver identify and access incompetence: They each enter a maladaptive (resourceless) state. The Receiver closes her eyes. The Pitcher offers a five-minute relaxation induction of hypnosis. If the Pitcher does not use hypnosis, she can offer progressive relaxation instructions or guided imagery.

Both the Pitcher and the Receiver access incompetent (resourceless) states in their respective roles. For example, the Pitcher acts passive or forgetful. The Receiver becomes agitated, aggressive, fails to listen, etc. Participants should choose one, and only one, incompetence. They do not openly share the orientation of resourcelessness they will portray. They must be specific and consistent in portraying their chosen incompetence. Also, the participants should become more incompetent progressively, i.e., develop the incompetence gradually over the course of the exercise until it is mildly exaggerated.

The Pitcher should be as competent as possible technically when offering the induction or progressive relaxation instructions, and use the best available method. The incompetence should primarily be an extra-verbal posture/state.

After the exercise, the partners incompetently guess their respective partner's state of being incompetent. Discussion can address the qualities involved that are central to the respective states. **The Phenomenology Table (page ____)** can be used. Participants can provide feedback to help their partner identify a core component, e.g., "What was most obvious when you were in your incompetent state was that you spoke rapidly."

The Pitcher and Receiver do not reverse roles until instructed to do so. When the exercise is completed the roles are reversed. In the second iteration, the Pitcher and Receiver select an incompetent state of one of their parents and develop it progressively over the course of the exercise. Again, in the discussion after the exercises, make an incompetent guess about the partner's state, and identify a core component.

Review: Participants must (a) select an incompetence; (b) stay specific in the task of portraying it; (c) develop it gradually and progressively, eventually exaggerating it; (d) make incompetent guesses about the incompetence of their partner; and (e) deconstruct their states after the exercise and find a core component.

Variations:

1. In the first iteration, the Pitchers and Receivers identify their mother's most common incompetent state and progressively act resourceless in the same way. The exercise is then repeated by identifying and exaggerating their father's primary incompetent state.
2. The Pitcher and Receiver role-play a therapy session or initial interview and act incompetent in their respective roles, perhaps using their parental positions of resourcelessness.
3. In a role-play, do incompetent EMDR, CBT, Gestalt therapy, coaching, psychological testing, etc.
4. In a role-play, portray incompetent parenting, business management, sports performance, supervision, marital relationship, etc.
5. Use in therapy and supervision. (See discussion.)

Purpose: To learn how to access, identify, and change states. To have fun while learning. To desensitize "incompetence." To realize that incompetence is a "family feeling" that may be inadvertently passed from generation to generation. Intentionally practicing states of incompetence can help to clear the pallet of the ingrained need to over strive for immediate competence.

Attitude: The ideal attitude for participating in the **PSYCHOAEROBIC**$_{SM}$ Exercises is playful, cooperative, and nonjudgmental.

PSYCHOAEROBIC$_{SM}$ Exercises are conducted to identify and access resource states. The exercises challenge people to discover strengths or weaknesses. They are not competitive events in which competency is judged.

Note: No class member should feel in any way obligated to participate in an exercise.

Discussion: Warm-up Exercise 1:

In a recent workshop, I demonstrated Warm-up Exercise 1 by using a progressive relaxation technique. I tried my best to ensure that the verbalizations were reasonably competent. The alteration was made in my state because I became increasingly self-absorbed in my attitude, gestures, and posture, eventually ignoring the client to focus on my own process of relaxation. The client took a posture of being dimwitted, increasingly asking irrelevant questions. At the end of the exercise, we made incompetent guesses. He surmised that I was passive. I guessed that he was overly intellectual.

Here are several reasons for starting with Warm-up Exercise 1:

1.) It sets a tone of having fun, which should permeate the practice of subsequent exercises.
2.) It underscores the essential purpose of the Psychoaerobic model, which centers on realizing concepts and modifying states. Some people are adept at changing states; others are not. Those who are not skillful can use this, or related formats and practice exercises in which flexibly changing states is the primary goal.
3.) It allows clinicians to examine potential areas of incompetence that may affect their job as a clinician in a setting that is safe and conducive for growth and development.
4.) This exercise is meant to eliminate "competence-driven" orientations, so that competence will no longer be a preoccupation in future exercises.
5.) Clinicians need to tolerate their own incompetence. It is a daunting task to offer psychotherapy and attempt to understand a patient's existential reality. Over striving for competence seems to be an occupational hazard for many aspiring clinicians. But, therapists are destined

to be incompetent a considerable percentage of the time.

Athletes learn to tolerate incidents and states of incompetence. Consider baseball. The on-base percentage is a measure of how often the batter reaches base for any reason other than an error. Approximately one-third of the time the average professional baseball player gets on base. That means two-thirds of the time an average professional baseball player is incompetent. The record for the highest on-base percentage is held by Ted Williams at .482. Although he is considered one of the greats of the game, his score shows that he was less than competent more than 50% of the time. Michael Jordan, arguably the greatest basketball player in history, missed more than 50% of his shots from the floor. Professional athletes are paid handsomely for being incompetent a majority of the time.

6.) There is an existential reason for extolling incompetence. We are trapped on a moving planet whose orbital speed is about 30 km/s (108,000 kilometers per hour). Our inaccurate sense of competence tells us that we are stationary. The sun around which our planet orbits is a peripheral star in a peripheral galaxy. There are at least 10^{11} known galaxies and approximately 10^{11} stars in each galaxy. If each star has 10 exoplanets, the number of planets in the universe approaches Avogadro's number. In addition, the universe is inexplicably accelerating after billions of years of decelerating. The origin of the universe, moreover, is open to question, but all galaxies, stars, and planets will eventually become extinct. Anyone who extols an inflated sense of competence under these existential conditions of abject uncertainty is in denial of delusional proportions. Our openly admitted incompetence keeps us humble.
7.) The first iteration of the exercise is projective. The reason that participants select a specific form of incompetence can be analyzed and understood.
8.) In the second iteration, participants are asked to select an incompetence of one of their parents. Oftentimes, the projected incompetent state from the first iteration is similar to, or is complementary with, the incompetence of the chosen parent in the second iteration. We do not invent our incompetence; it is a family inheritance subcon-

sciously passed from generation to generation.

9.) Patients in psychotherapy present because of troublesome, incompetent states. A therapist could interpret the patient's incompetence as a historical remnant from a previous generation. Perhaps that interpretation would lead to change. But, the best way to stimulate conceptual realizations is by using experiential methods. When I suggest being experiential to aspiring therapists, they are often at a loss for specifics about how to be experiential. It would be possible to adapt Warm-up Exercise 1 within the context of a therapeutic consultation. Envision these steps: The patient is instructed to choose an incompetence and then plan to cook a meal demonstrating the incompetence. Next, the client is instructed to incompetently plan a meal, this time using an incompetence of one of his parents. Then, the patient is asked to reflect on the difference between the chosen incompetence and the parental incompetence. This experiential procedure may lead the client to self-discover the etiology of his incompetence. Such experiential insight will likely be more powerful than a therapist's interpretation.

10.) The exercise can be modified by a therapist offering family therapy who wants to make an intervention experiential. Take a hypothetical, super-competent family. Father enters the room in a perfectly appointed business suit, steeples his hands, and sits in a classic male "T" posture. Mother is dressed tastefully and crosses her legs at the ankles. The little girl wears a white dress and her hair is neatly pulled back. Then...the adolescent boy enters the room with spiked hair, tattoos, and piercings. He is wearing an ill-fitting, graphic T-shirt and tattered jeans that are falling off his hips. He invents a position of sitting in a chair that has no historical precedent. Although it would be easy for a therapist to comment on a discrepancy of values, I doubt that such obvious intervention would lead to change. Perhaps Warm-up Exercise 1 could be modified. The family could be given a homework assignment or an in-session task of incompetently planning a family outing in which everyone would participate. The adolescent could be put in charge. Such staging could lead the family to make an interpretation about their structure and predicament, which could be instrumental in evoking change, because it is stimulated from the inside rather than presented from the outside.

11.) Learning any new method is usually a process of trial and error. When learning a new technique of therapy, whether hypnosis, CBT, or EMDR, a student can be instructed to incompetently role-play it. This assignment may be effective, especially for those students who over strive for competence, which then impedes learning.

EXPERIENTIAL EMPOWERMENT
PSYCHOAEROBIC$_{SM}$ Exercises
www.psychoaerobic.org

WARM-UP EXERCISE 2

Clinician Posture to Develop: A resource state: emotional expression; emotional range; and the use of one's body to communicate.

Format: Circle of six to eight people.

Roles: Each person serves as both Pitcher and Receiver.

Method: The first Pitcher says a gibberish sentence consisting of three or four gibberish words to the person on her immediate right, who then becomes the Receiver. The Receiver takes the last gibberish word she heard and says it back to the Pitcher, but adds to the repetition by conveying a specific emotion, such as surprise, joy, sadness, etc.

It is also possible for the Receiver to add an emotion and reflect back the entire gibberish sentence. The Receiver then becomes the new Pitcher and composes a new sentence of three or four gibberish words. The new Receiver then takes the last gibberish word (or the entire phrase) she heard, and repeats it conveying an emotion that was not previously used. The exercise continues around the group so that each participant has one or more turns.

Here's an example:

Person One to Person Two: Iton erdlu blecka.

Person Two back to Person One: Blecka!

Person Two to Person Three: Wanta slip nooden.

Person Three back to Person Two: Nooden?

Person Three to Person Four: Perca redop lento.

Person Four back to Person Three: Lento?!

Person Four to Person Five: Reno melton porlap.

Variations:

1. The Receiver repeats the gibberish sentence exactly as it was presented, mirroring back the Pitcher's gesture, tone, and tempo.
2. The gibberish sentence is designed to express a specific emotion. The Receiver identifies in one gibberish word the underlying emotion of the Pitcher's gibberish. Then the Receiver becomes the new Pitcher. Alternatively, the Receiver can exaggerate the underlying emotion of the Pitcher by reflecting it back and enhancing it, e.g., "Glat!" can be mirrored as "GLAT!!" The Receiver then presents a new gibberish sentence to the next person, but adds in an emotion that was not used previously.
3. The gibberish sentences said to the subsequent Receiver are composed to suggest relaxation, enthusiasm, etc. The group leader calls out goals (e.g., relaxation, enthusiasm, or curiosity), and the participants modify their gibberish sentence accordingly.
4. Speak gibberish "depression," "anxiety," etc.
5. Each member of the group takes a turn at speaking gibberish depression (or anxiety) in order to experience variations, which can later be discussed.
6. "Telephone" version: The first Pitcher provides a gibberish sentence and complementary gesture, and the Receiver mirrors it back. Then, the new Pitcher turns to the next Receiver and repeats the first Pitcher's sentence and gesture. The group repeats the process until the sentence is returned to the initial Pitcher. Be sure to pass along the exact phrase, tone, and gesture you receive just as you perceive it from your Pitcher. Do not correct it to resemble the initial presentation. Circle around the group once or twice. The telephone version can also be conducted in slow motion.

Purpose: To develop emotional range.

Attitude: The ideal attitude for participating in **PSYCHOAEROBIC**$_{SM}$ Exercises is playful, cooperative, and nonjudgmental.

Adapted from an exercise that appears in Keith Johnstone's *IMPRO: Improvisation and the Theatre.*

Discussion: Warm-up Exercise 2:

Using gibberish may seem daunting at first, but there are good reasons for using it. Gibberish has its place in training actors. For example, if the actors are overly focused on saying their lines, they may miss some of the important subtleties of emotional expression. A director, therefore, may have the actors practice the scene in gibberish during rehearsal as a means to access subtleties. Through this exercise, actors can focus on the nonverbal aspects of communication, the emotional intent of the dialogue, and responses from the other actors in the scene. Singers can practice similarly. They may first use syllables to learn the music so that they can eventually convey the intervals and tones that project the intended feeling.

The founder of Gestalt therapy, Fritz Perls, used gibberish in his practice of group therapy. I listened to a tape of Perls in his later years in which he asked group members to speak gibberish. The anxiety created by this unexpected exercise brought to the surface underlying "neurotic" conflicts that existed in participants. Honing in on the emerging difficulties, Perls used them as a focus for therapy.

I remember an incident in which Milton Erickson used gibberish with me. To my surprise and delight, after first visiting him, I was invited to the wedding of his youngest daughter, which was to take place at his home. The unexpected invitation arrived shortly after our initial meeting. I do not recall expecting to visit him again after our first encounter. It was only much later that I realized Dr. Erickson had a way of re-parenting, in which patients and students would become Erickson "family members" for a while, and then eventually "graduate" and leave "home."

During the reception, I cornered Dr. Erickson in his kitchen and awkwardly asked him a professional question. Yes, I was young and naïve. He smiled softly, and then replied with a gibberish phrase. Noting how perplexed I was, he playfully uttered more gibberish. Stupefied, I looked quizzically at him. Again, he smiled and spoke even more gibberish. Eventually, Mrs. Erickson intervened, saying, "Oh Milton, stop that." Suddenly I realized that the wedding celebration was for play, not education. Consistent with his style, Dr. Erickson made the moment experiential. I did not feel chastised as I might have if he had he said directly to me, "This is a celebration, not a time for supervision."

Introducing the concept of using gibberish as a Warm-up Exercise has other value: Some of the Psychoaerobic Exercises that follow rely upon the method of using gibberish and can be used in psychotherapy and supervision. Practicing communication with gibberish is a useful tool for communicating in general because gains in confidence and flexibility, and it can be used in many professional and nonprofessional settings.

A useful group exercise for children diagnosed as ADHD can be based in gibberish. The therapist creates flash cards with the name of an emotion on each one, such as anger or disappointment. Two cards are given to one child, who serves as the leader in that round. Without openly naming the emotions, the child is instructed to separately act out each emotion using gibberish. The other children in the group can guess each emotion. In this game, children learn about emotional expression and the art of reading others' emotions, skills that are often lacking in children with an ADHD diagnosis. Similar exercises can be devised for adults who have problems with emotional expression and understanding.

I have used gibberish in couples therapy. Consider the couple for whom escalating fights is a habitual pastime. When they stage a fight in the consulting room, I might ask them to re-enact the fight in gibberish. A number of salutary consequences may arise. The couple may realize their demeaning tones or behaviors: "I didn't realize how disrespectful it was to point at you like that." Or, the couple may break into spontaneous laughter, realizing the absurdity of their fight. This exercise may also serve as a "computer virus." When the couple remembers it at home, it can disrupt a typical, programmed fight. There is another factor: The use of gibberish may be appropriate for symbolic reasons. It is often the case that the content of the fight is gibberish anyway, and speaking gibberish may unearth the emotional subtext.

I have used gibberish in family therapy to stimulate playfulness. A disengaged family might be asked to only speak gibberish during the course of a dinner. A similar exercise could be used for disengaged couples.

Gibberish can also be used in individual therapy. I remember an example in which Dr. Erickson learned the word salad pattern of a schizophrenic patient, and then used it to establish rapport. The tailored, world salad conversation led the patient to feel respected. Eventually, this method allowed the patient to initiate more coherent conversation.

Gibberish can be valuable for students. Rather than memorizing the DSM components of a psychiatric malady, the student could use gibberish and role-play a problem, such as depression or anxiety. Subsequent discussion could elucidate the student's realization of the components of the diagnosis. Student realizations may be more effective as a learning tool than rote memorization of DSM dimensions.

A student who is learning techniques of relaxation training could offer instructions to a mock patient in gibberish during a role-play, thereby experiencing and conceptualizing the nonverbal and paraverbal elements of the technique. The same could be done for learning systematic desensitization or hypnosis.

Again, there is an essential principle that underlies the experiential method: *Dynamic experiences can precede dynamic understandings*. Experiential methods enliven the moment and can foster desirable outcomes.

EXPERIENTIAL EMPOWERMENT
PSYCHOAEROBIC$_{SM}$ Exercises
www.psychoaerobic.org

WARM-UP EXERCISE 3

Clinician Posture to Develop: Resource states of empathic attunement (resonance) and experiential assessment.

Format: Group of five to eight participants.

Roles: One person is the Pitcher; the others are Receivers.

Method: The Pitcher tells an emotional and personally revealing secret in four or five sentences, but speaks subvocally, using normal gestures, postures, and facial expressions. The person does not pantomime. He mouths the words using complete sentences, but does not speak aloud. The secret can be negative, such as something terribly shameful, or it can be positive, such as a profound intimate experience. The secret needs to evoke strong emotions.

The Receivers attend and allow their bodies to empathically resonate with the Pitcher's emotion. The Receivers should stay kinetic, moving constantly in response to their body's intuitive perception of the Pitcher's emotions. Cognitive processing to determine the emotions should be limited as much as possible. The Receiver's body can seamlessly portray the feeling of the Pitcher. The empathic assessment of emotion is realized by the Receiver's responsive postures.

The Receivers do not look directly at the teller of the secret. They use indirect eye contact or peripheral vision only, perhaps focusing on the Pitcher's knee and watching with a soft focus. When the Pitcher finishes telling the secret, then and only then, will the Receivers freeze and become statues. Maintaining a stylized posture they hold their final pose so that the Pitcher can see each Receiver's physical portrayal of empathy. The group members can also look at each other's statues to see how other group members resonated, but, movements should be minimal and the final pose should remain unchanged as much as possible. The Receivers should not openly guess the emotion behind the secret.

The next Pitcher tells a secret and the Receivers "resonate" with the Pitcher's emotion. It may be beneficial for the Pitchers and Receiver to do something physical between sets to de-role—stretch, walk around the room, etc.

Variations:

1. Tell an emotional story rather than a secret.
2. Conduct the exercise in dyads.
3. Tell the secret in gibberish, rather than subvocally.
4. Tell the secret using only one syllable, such as "Bah," "Ru," or "Lee."
5. The Receiver(s) can guess the emotion, naming it in one word.
6. The Receiver(s) can gently mirror the Pitcher as a technique to discern the underlying emotion. To avoid making the Pitcher self-conscious, three methods can be used:
   (a) The Leader secretly provides mirroring instructions to Receivers prior to the exercise.
   (b) Use a one-second delay before mirroring.
   (c) Obscure the mirroring by using approximations. (If the Pitcher makes an open gesture, the Receivers minimally open their posture.)
7. Each person successively describes his or her state of empathic attunement after completing the entire exercise. "I know I was empathically attuned because I ______." I know I was empathically attuned when I _________." The States Table can be used.

Purpose: To develop a state of implicit emotional resonance/ empathetic attunement. To develop experiential empathy.

Attitude: The ideal attitude for participating in **PSYCHOAEROBIC$_{SM}$** Exercises is playful, cooperative, and nonjudgmental.

Discussion: Warm-up Exercise 3

A skill set that underlies all schools of therapy is empathic attunement. Customarily, graduate students are taught verbal methods of overtly demonstrating their understanding of the emotional understructure of the client's message. Empathic listening skills are good as a starting point for effective clinical work, and they can add depth to any relationship. But, empathy can also be demonstrated in the posture that the clinician naturally assumes, making empathy experiential rather than verbal.

Listening is only one way to detect emotional subtext. Sometimes the therapist's body has a degree of empathic attunement that precedes (and supersedes) the therapist's cognitive understanding; it may be a powerful indicator of the emotional understructure.

In Warm-up Exercise 3, the emphasis is on the experience of the Receiver, not the Pitcher. Imagine similarly pitched tuning forks in a conductive environment. If one of the tuning forks is struck, the other will resonate. It is the job of the Receivers to serve as resonant tuning forks, allowing their bodies to respond to the emotional energy of the Pitcher.

As I have matured as a therapist, I have become more attuned to my body's understanding of therapeutic moments. With some patients, I find myself sitting rigidly. Then I become aware that the sensitivities of the patient are so great that any "aberrant" movement by me creates dissonance. This type of patient may have many implicit relational requirements for how the therapist "must" behave. Often it is the case that the greater the patient's problem, the more relational requirements are placed on the therapist.

Imagine yourself as a life coach or clinician. At certain times you may lean forward in an open position, arms outstretched with palms up. Or, you might find yourself pulling back and crossing your arms tightly against your chest. What is happening in the interaction that leads your body to respond in these ways? Perhaps by monitoring your body's reaction, you can utilize it to facilitate goals. By checking in with your body, you may get a deeper understanding of the patient's internal environment.

This exercise can be modified in therapy sessions with patients (individual, group, or family) who would benefit from empathic attunement, for example, a narcissistic client or disengaged teenager. It can be used with children in a group setting as a game to teach attunement.

Sometimes a patient has an embarrassing secret that he is reluctant to divulge to a therapist. The sub-verbal method outlined in Warm-up Exercise 3 could be used (or the patient could tell the secret in gibberish, or only using a nonsense syllable), thereby meeting both sides of the patient's ambivalence — the need to tell the secret, and the need to withhold it.

There is an additional implication that can be derived from this exercise. Verbally expressing empathy is effective, but the technique can be improved. A posture (or an expression, or gesture) can be strategically employed to visually communicate empathetic understanding. A posture is more experiential and conceptual than a verbal reflection of empathy, and it may be more powerful. A posture is more a state of being, than a verbal reaction. A posture is "living empathy," or experiential empathy. Adding experiential components will strengthen therapeutic interventions in almost any school of therapy. Making an intervention visual is more memorable than a verbal comment.

EXPERIENTIAL EMPOWERMENT
PSYCHOAEROBIC$_{SM}$ Exercises
www.psychoaerobic.org

WARM-UP EXERCISE 4

Clinician Posture to Develop: To prime analogical and symbolic thinking.

Format: Group (any size) — each person with paper and pencil.

Method: Each person accesses his or her essential (most central) posture/state as a clinician. The group leader then asks participants to describe themselves as a clinician using analogies. "As a clinician, what color would you be?" "As a clinician, what animal would you be?" Here's a list of possible categories for analogies:

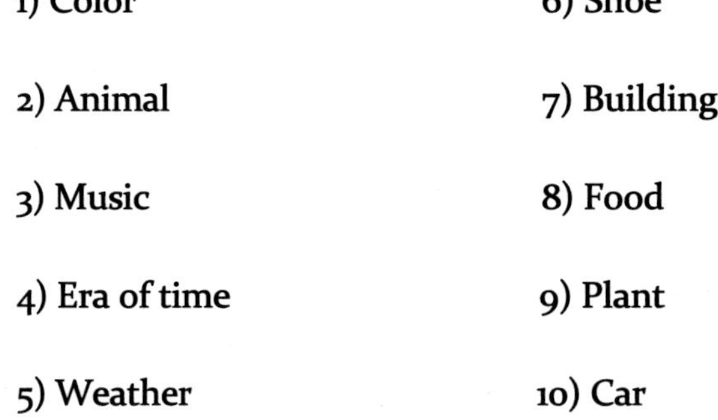

1) Color	**6) Shoe**
2) Animal	**7) Building**
3) Music	**8) Food**
4) Era of time	**9) Plant**
5) Weather	**10) Car**

The description is written, kept, and does not need to be shared with the group.

Once the exercise has been completed, participants can reflect on the state they were in when creating analogies, perhaps describing a central phenomenological component of the state to a partner.

Variations:

1. To establish a symbolic baseline.
2. For team building. (See the exercise discussion.)
3. To create analogical solutions, e.g., for problems like pain.
4. To be used as an assessment device for a client in describing:
   (a) Symptom(s) — If your symptom was a color, what color would it be?
   (b) Personal strengths — If your personal strength was a color, what color would it be? What color would you be if you were at your best as a romantic partner, employee, golfer?
   (c) The quality of the immediate social system — If your family was a color, what color would it be? If your work team was a color, what color would it be?
   (d) Individual members of the family or social system. If your husband was a color, what color would he be? If your boss was a color, what color would he be?
   (e) Social role – As a teacher, student, parent, etc., what color would you be?

Purpose: To develop the state of being "metaphoric."

Discussion: Warm-up Exercise 4

The seeming simplicity of this exercise is deceptive. It possesses depth that is not obvious at first, and it offers opportunities for useful permutations.

To establish a symbolic baseline and barometer of change, I have used this exercise at the beginning of Psychoaerobic workshops. I ask students to complete the exercise, and then put it away. At the end of the workshop, I ask them to do the exercise again and compare it with the first iteration. Analogical changes can indicate growth. This version could be used similarly in psychotherapy or in business coaching.

Warm-up Exercise 4 could be modified for team building. Each member of the team can fill out the form describing him- or herself as a team member. The descriptions would be collected by the leader who then begins with the phrase, "Which team member is______?" and then reads the descriptors written by each team member so that others can guess which member fits the description.

I have used variations of this exercise when working with patients with chronic pain. I begin by asking patients to indicate Subjective Units of Distress Scale (SUDS) using a 10-point scale, where 10 is the highest; zero the lowest. There might be two scales — one for pain, and one for suffering caused by the pain. (Alternatively, I might use a scale to indicate the level of comfort.) I then ask patients to describe their pain analogically, perhaps using the following descriptors: color, plant, tool, and vessel containing water. I might repeat the list three times, expecting that with each iteration there will be a change. Perhaps the first iteration from the patient includes the following descriptors: red, Saguaro cactus, sledge hammer, and tub. The third repetition might reflect change, and be reported as follows: orange, thorny rosebush, ball-peen hammer, and pitcher. Most patients report a change over the course of the iterations, perhaps because of my expectation, perhaps because of the use of analogies, perhaps because of the alteration of attention prompted by the exercise. Subsequently, I might ask the patient, while in hypnosis, to envision a pitcher with orange liquid. In his imagination, the client is asked to use the hammer to tap a small hole in the pitcher and watch the liquid as it drains out. The rosebush can be planted in the pitcher. Thereafter, SUDS could be used to indicate the level of pain and the level of suffering (or the level of comfort). Metaphorical solutions can be surprisingly effective.

There are myriad ways to use the exercise as an assessment device, which will establish and/or alter the future treatment plan. After all, a treatment plan unfolds due to assessment. The exercise could be used in an initial session, where the client could be asked to describe problems or strengths using analogies. Having such lists in hand would facilitate the creation of therapeutic metaphors.

In couples therapy the partners could describe themselves and each other using analogies. The therapeutic purpose might be to increase connection. The instructions can be slightly modified: At your best as a couple, what color/animal/fabric are you? At your best as an intimate partner, what color would you be? The analogies could also be used by the couple in their day-to-day conversation to playfully elicit goals states at home: "I would appreciate it if you would be more 'green' right now."

In a workshop I conducted for trainers, the exercise was modified thusly: At your best as a teacher, what color (or other variable) would you be? At your best as a student, what color (or other variable) would you be?

There is an overarching reason for using this exercise to develop therapist states. As previously indicated, metaphor can be used to empower emotional impact. To develop a state of being metaphoric, clinicians can start by using analogies. As I have matured as a therapist and teacher, the density and frequency of my use of analogies and metaphor have increased to the satisfaction of my clients and students, because being metaphoric prompts experiential realizations.

EXPERIENTIAL EMPOWERMENT
PSYCHOAEROBIC$_{SM}$ Exercises
www.psychoaerobic.org

WARM-UP EXERCISE 5

Clinician Posture to Develop: Being experiential.

Format: Group of five or six participants in a circle.

Roles: Each person, in turn, becomes a Pitcher.

Method: Each participant throws one shoe into the center of the circle, and then takes someone else's shoe out of the circle and tries to put it on. In turn, each participant tries desperately to make the chose shoe fit. In turn, participants describe how or why they are trying to make the shoe fit, even though it is obvious it does not fit. Descriptions should be five to 10 sentences that start with the sentence stem, "I am desperately trying to make this shoe fit by ____________," or "I am desperately trying to make this shoe fit because ____________."

Variation: Conduct the exercise in pairs. One person role-plays the Counselor and the other plays the Client. The Counselor gives his shoe to the Client who uses the method outlined above. After each description/rationale, the Counselor attempts to dissuade the Client from continuing the fruitless activity. The Client continues with her attempts, all the while providing reasons for doing so. Perhaps the Counselor can use experiential approaches to try to deter the Client from senseless action. For example, the Counselor can senselessly make repetitive tapping sounds until the Client realizes the futility of his actions. Perhaps the Counselor can reflect back the Client's reasoning in a soft voice.

Purpose: To experientially realize the agitation and rationalizations in which clients often engage.

Discussion: Warm-up Exercise 5

It is common for people to agitate themselves by senselessly repeating ineffective patterns. At first glance, it may seem like something constructive is happening because there is so much activity, but upon further investigation, it becomes evident that chapno substantial changes ensue. Agitation is a passive behavior because it does not solve the problem; it simply turns back on itself.

Attempts by counselors to interrupt such behavior may be unsuccessful. Simple, experiential interventions can be helpful. The justification for ineffective behavior is usually instrumental in maintaining patterns. If the client (or clinician) recites the justification openly, with small modifications (using a soft voice, for example), change can result. Once, when I was working with a patient who incessantly dithered about a problem, I started tapping on my head. The patient looked at me quizzically. I continued tapping. "Do you know why I continue tapping myself on the head?" I asked. When she inquired, I told her, "I am doing it because...it feels so good when I stop." The client laughed...and stopped her agitation. An experiential intervention can be more powerful than a verbal confrontation.

EXPERIENTIAL EMPOWERMENT
PSYCHOAEROBIC$_{SM}$ Exercises
www.psychoaerobic.org

WARM-UP EXERCISE 6

Hot Potato

Clinician Posture to Develop: To playfully learn modeling skills. To promote creativity.

Format: Circle of six to eight people.

Roles: Each person in turn serves as a Pitcher and Receiver.

Method: The first Pitcher assumes a hand and arm gesture that represents an emotion, concept, or state, and holds it for a few seconds. The gesture can be static or kinetic. Then, she "tosses it" to another member of the group who holds the gesture for a few seconds to fully experience it. The Receiver then makes a new gesture and tosses it to another group member. Receivers must hold the gesture thrown to them for a few seconds before shifting to a new one.

To get the most out of this exercise, do it methodically. Unlike the children's game "hot potato," the goal is not about quick reflexes, but rather about realizing different states and emotions. Vary the gestures to represent different emotions and states that are both positive and negative. Try doing the exercise in slow motion in order to facilitate deeper understanding of the power of gestures to convey emotions.

Variations:

1. Play "faceball." Rather than using a gesture, make a facial expression that conveys an emotion/state, then "throw" the facial expression to a member of the group. The Receiver holds the facial expression for a moment, then creates a different expression, and

subsequently throws it to another participant who repeats the process.

2. Pass postures that represent emotions around the group rather than gestures.
3. Pass emotional movements around the group, such as clapping appreciatively, or signaling to someone to move closer.
4. Pass emotional sounds around the group, such as whimpering, groaning, etc.
5. Pass postures and gestures that symbolize problems.
6. Pass posture and gestures that symbolize resources.
7. The group leader calls out an emotion or state, which the Pitcher molds into a gesture and then
"throws" to a member of the group, who then becomes the next Pitcher. Then, the group leader calls out another emotion or state.
8. Toss an imaginary ball among group members. Try *not* to be creative for as long as possible.

Purpose: To expand the state of emotional expression. To realize implicit creativity.

Discussion: Warm-up Exercise 6

This exercise can be used with patients and students to enhance playfulness, emotional expression, and emotional understanding. Representing emotions with facial or body gestures, sounds, and more, can be especially effective in expressing deep, empathetic understanding. This exercise can be used in group or family therapy to promote engagement.

Therapists can strategically express emotions using gestures, sounds, facial expression, etc. in order to affect therapy. Rather than suggesting to a client that it would be valuable to act assertively, the therapist can indicate: "Perhaps you can act ...," creating a gesture that indicates an assertive stance.

Creativity is a byproduct of human interaction. The variation (#8) in which creativity is restricted invariably provides the experiential realization that it is impossible to restrict creativity.

EXPERIENTIAL EMPOWERMENT
PSYCHOAEROBIC$_{SM}$ Exercises
www.psychoaerobic.org

WARM-UP EXERCISE 7

Clinician Posture to Develop: Using analogies and living metaphors.

Format: Several small groups, each standing in a circle.

Roles: Each person is a Pitcher and Receiver.

Method: When prompted, a participant locates a source of distress in a specific place in her body. The first person, the Pitcher, points to a place in her body where she houses a resourceless state, for example, depression, agitation, confusion, passivity. She points, but does not name the resourceless state. Next, she pantomimes taking the resourceless state out of her body and while holding it in her hands, she describes it. The resourceless state can be described analogically in terms of shape, size, color, strength, etc. The description should consist of five to 10 words. Then the Pitcher "passes" the resourceless state to the next person who becomes the Receiver. The Receiver holds the resourceless state in her hands for a few moments, honoring it and appreciating it. The Receiver then ceremoniously gets up and places the resourceless state somewhere in the room. The Receiver then becomes the next Pitcher and the exercise is continued until all participants have a turn serving as Pitcher and Receiver.

Time is reserved for discussion after the exercise has been completed by all group members. Discuss the phenomenology of the states of the participants that are accessed in the exercise — in portraying their resourceless states, receiving them, and in placing them somewhere in the room.

Variations:

1. Instead of pointing to a resourceless state and taking it in hand, the Pitcher assumes a posture (sculpture) that represents the resourceless state, and then describes it analogically to the group in five to 10 descriptive words. An example: "My sculpture is heavy, unbalanced, blue, and mushy." The Pitcher takes time to adequately explore the posture of the resourceless state before listing the descriptors. Then, the person to the right is asked to mirror the posture of that resourcesless state. This person assumes it for a few moments, and then adds some descriptors, indicating qualities she feels when assuming the posture.
2. The Pitcher provides as many descriptions of the resourceless state as there are people in the group. The Pitcher sequentially projects each description onto one group member after another, e.g., if the Pitcher first describes the resourceless state as "heavy," she tells the first group member, "You are heavy." The group members can pantomime representing the descriptor. It should be emphasized to the group members that the projection is the Pitcher's and has no relevance to individuals in the group.
3. The exercise can be done in pairs with a variation: The Pitcher identifies the resourceless state of her father and repeats the exercise from that perspective. For example, the Pitcher holds it in her hands or sculpts it, describes it, then passes it to the partner who is the Receiver. The exercise is repeated from the perspective of the mother. Then the pair switches roles.
4. The participants place the extracted resourceless states ceremoniously, one by one, in the center of the circle. Upon completing the exercise, they collectively construct something imaginary with the "resourceless" objects. Perhaps they build a tower, or create a garden or museum.
5. The participants increase the scope and intensity of the resourceless state before removing it, perhaps by exaggerating some characteristic of it analogically or behaviorally.
6. The Receivers at first feign an inability to remove their resourceless state. Then they exaggerate and perhaps provide rationale for their inability.

Purpose: To experience the state of being metaphoric. Symbolic actions strengthen realizations.

Discussion: Warm-up Exercise 7

We are an amalgamation of strengths and weaknesses, assets and liabilities, and positive and negative patterns and states. There can be constructive aspects to perceived deficits. A problem state in one context may be a solution state in another. A present liability may have been a historical strength. Weaknesses may have hidden aspects that can be utilized. Problems have an energy that can be harnessed constructively. Prior to making a change, sometimes it is optimal to first appreciate and honor the negative pattern. At other times, change can be initiated by exaggerating the problem state. By nature, human beings are symbolic, and symbolic actions hold great sway in human interaction. Externalizing a perceived flaw can be an effective step in promoting change. Externalization (a method espoused by narrative therapists) can be accomplished experientially. Seeing one's problems portrayed analogically by another can be beneficial.

In one variation, the resourceless state is first symbolically increased. Any change in a habitual pattern can lead to constructive alterations. If a problem can be made worse, it can be made better. In another variation, components of the resourceless state are externalized and projected individually to group members. Cleaving a problem into manageable units can be an effective strategy.

WARM-UP EXERCISE 8

Clinician Posture to Develop: To prime analogical and symbolic thinking; to note the effect of gesture on state; to improve body awareness; to experience the systemic effect of a minimal change; and to build on the positive.

Format: Group. In turn, each person serves as Pitcher.

Method: The first Pitcher assumes a stylized posture representing an answer to the question, "At your best, who are you as a clinician?" The Pitcher's posture or "sculpture" can be static or dynamic. The Pitcher thinks of a word or phrase that best describes the essence of the posture. The descriptor, which should be announced to the group, becomes a title for the sculpture. The title is placed somewhere in relationship to the sculpture, and its qualities are described: "My title is over my head. It is made of wooden letters painted black. The letters are in Times New Roman and each letter is about 5 inches tall."

Subsequently, the group asks the Pitcher to change one small aspect of the sculpture that could enhance it, e.g., slightly shifting one leg. The group members should privately consult with one another before suggesting each posture change. The group should ask the Pitcher to make a minimal change that they believe will be systemically significant; they try to make the smallest change that will enhance the Pitcher's state. When asked, the Pitcher indicates whether or not the modified posture significantly changes the title. A change in the title is accepted as signifying a change in state. If not, the group members again consult with each other privately, and suggest another alteration. When the sculpture is significantly changed, as indicated by a change in the title, the Pitcher can memorize the new posture, and use the amended title as an anchor to enter the more ideal state when seeing patients. The Pitcher can announce the title of the new sculpture to the group and/or describe characteristics of the new title: "My new title is in 10-inch Helvetica and it is made of gold and it is now positioned directly in front of me."

When the exercise is completed, the states that are accessed and the processes of change are discussed. Then, the next person in the group takes a turn as Pitcher.

Variations: Use in individual, group, couples or family therapy. Use in coaching and supervision.

Purpose: To be in the state of being both systemic and metaphoric.

Discussion: Warm-up Exercise 8

In therapy, this exercise can be conducted with a couple or with a family, and then discussed (as therapeutically indicated). In an initial session of couples therapy, each partner can take a turn at creating a mutual sculpture to represent their ideal relationship. Alternatively, each partner can separately sculpt him- or herself into a representation of being the best partner possible. Titles can be created for the sculptures. In consultation with the therapist, the partners can think of ways their sculptures can be minimally improved. Sometimes it is most effective if change is incremental. A small change can have a systemic effect.

Each subsequent clinical session could commence by having the clients assume their ideal posture, cuing it with its title. Alternatively, the therapist can strategically assume the desired posture to demonstrate it to the clients. The possible permutations of this exercise are endless, and can be modified according to predilections and circumstances.

EXPERIENTIAL EMPOWERMENT
PSYCHOAEROBIC$_{SM}$ Exercises
www.psychoaerobic.org

WARM-UP EXERCISE 9

Clinician Posture to Develop: Identifying and changing states.

Format: Dyads. Each person has paper and pencil.

Roles: One Pitcher; one Receiver.

Method: The Pitcher gives 10 sincere compliments to the Receiver. The Receiver silently rejects the compliments and responds by becoming progressively more defensive with each compliment. The Receiver eventually enters a "defensive state." This can be accomplished physically, emotionally, behaviorally, with sounds, etc., but primarily it should be done nonverbally.

Subsequently, the Pitcher interviews the Receiver, asking, "Specifically, how do you know that you are defensive?" Responses can be behavioral, emotional, cognitive, symbolic, sensory, perceptual, attitudinal, temporal, gestural, postural, vocal, linguistic, energetic, relational, etc. The Receiver can prompt responses in different areas, e.g., "What specifically in your behavior lets you know that you're defensive? What specifically in your thinking?" The Pitcher can compose a written list of five to 10 important aspects of the defensive state. The Receiver maintains the defensive state.

Using his list, the Pitcher asks the Receiver to progressively eliminate the descriptions: "You know that you are defensive because your arms are folded across your chest. Unfold your arms. Are you still defensive?" If the defensiveness persists, the Pitcher continues until the Receiver has removed all cues, or until the Receiver reports that he is no longer defensive.

The roles are then reversed. This time the new Receiver accepts the compliments and enters a state of being self-assured. The same procedures are followed.

Discuss the states, their components, and the process of change.

Variations:

1. The Pitcher asks the Receiver to eliminate responses successively, rather than listing them first on paper. It is best for the Pitcher to start with minimal requests, beginning with cues that seem peripheral. The Pitcher can work progressively to cues that are more central. The Pitcher continues to make requests until the Receiver can no longer maintain either defensiveness or self-esteem.
2. The Pitcher induces a trance and follows the same procedures, e.g., "Specifically, how do you know that you are in a trance?" Then the Pitcher progressively removes cues.
3. The Receiver accesses the defensive/self-assured state by using memories, rather than compliments. Then the Pitcher sequentially suggests removing perceived elements until the state can no longer be maintained.
4. Other states, e.g., fear or anger, can be accessed in response to compliments.
5. Rather than using compliments, the Pitcher can use descriptions or neutral observations, e.g., "Your hair is brown." "The room is warm." The Receiver becomes defensive (or self-assured).

Purpose: To actualize states by exploring their elements. A state is an amalgamation, not an entity. Minimal change can have a systemic effect.

Discussion: Warm-up Exercise 9

This exercise was adopted from a historical study of hypnosis in which the investigator successively removed perceived phenomenological components from a hypnotized subject in an attempt to discover the essential nature of trance.

Understanding components can be useful in eliciting states. States can be understood as constructs of convenience. We name them as units and simplify a complex amalgamation for the heuristic purposes of understanding and communicating. For example, the states of motivation, or openness, or faith, or hypnosis are dimensional, composed of varying degrees of thoughts, feelings, behaviors, sensations, perceptions, patterns of attention, attitudes, energy flows, temporal aspects, postures, gestures, vocal characteristics, memories, linguistic patterns, contextual determinants, and relational characteristics. States, moreover, are fluid and change with time.

A state can be redintegrated from partial cues: Access and actualize a sufficient threshold of components and the state "just happens." Attempts at accessing the state directly may be less effective. Single cues can elicit a state; however, single cues may not be sufficient. By accessing a sufficient number of cues the state will "spontaneously" emerge.

Context alone may be a sufficient cue to enter a state. Step into a church or temple and you may experience reverence. A gesture can be a sufficient partial cue. Raise your head a bit and expose your throat, and you may feel vulnerable. Slow your tempo and you may become thoughtful. Focus your attention and you may feel mesmerized. Take on vocal and linguistic characteristics of your early childhood and you may become playful. Vividly review past mistakes and you may feel like a failure. Move closer to a person and you may feel intimacy.

Exiting from a state can sometimes be achieved by altering a single component. More commonly, however, there is a threshold that must be reached: By altering a significant number of components, the state will eventually lose its integrity.

In a classroom demonstration, I demonstrated this exercise with the concept of status. The class already understood that I was in a state of status because I was the teacher. I asked them to identify indicators that I had status, stating that I would eliminate them sequentially. In response to their suggestions, I put the microphone down, stopped talking, sat with my back to the group, and made any reasonable change that was requested. Eventually, I could no longer maintain a state of status. Having experienced the exercise a number of times, it is often the case that I lose status when I am asked to lower my head and slant it to one side.

But there is an additional change that immediately affected my ability to maintain status. One of the students wisely explained that I had status because the students in the class *gave* me status. When I asked students to stop affording me status by no longer attending to me, my state changed; I could no longer maintain status. I use this example to demonstrate the power of systemic and contextual alterations to alter states and concepts.

Warm-up Exercise 9 can be used in therapy and supervision. When working with a psychologically insightful client, this process can be used in a session. With a patient in a depressed or anxious "state," ask for specific descriptions, and then eliminate them successively as described in the exercise. Or, a homework assignment might be to alter components. For example, if the patient knows he is depressed because of his limited gestures and expressions in social situations, the homework assignment of being more expressive with his friends could be given. *The therapeutic heuristic is to make the smallest change that will have a systemic effect in altering the maladaptive state, and eliciting a more effective state.*

This exercise can be used with a couple or family. As an assessment device, have members make neutral observations about each other and discover what state they access. The sensitivities of close relationships can be so volatile that even an innocent compliment or a neutral description can create dissonance.

The exercise can be used for supervision and therapist development. Rather than viewing the profession of therapist as a social role, it could be considered a state. After assuming the state of therapist, components can be successively eliminated or added. Using this approach, the state of the therapist can be better understood, and then improved.

EXPERIENTIAL EMPOWERMENT
PSYCHOAEROBIC$_{SM}$ Exercises
www.psychoaerobic.org

WARM-UP EXERCISE 10

Clinician Posture to Develop: Understanding behavioral incongruities and their effect.

Format: Dyads.

Roles: One Pitcher; one Receiver.

Method: The Receivers are told to do their best to enter a trance/relaxed state during the ensuing exercise. Then they are dismissed from the room so that instructions can be given to the Pitcher.

Once the Receiver has returned, the Pitcher offers a five-minute progressive relaxation induction. (Alternative: active imagination can be used, and the Pitcher can suggest vividly experiencing being at the beach or walking in the country.)

When the Receiver is outside the room, the Pitcher is given an additional task — to impede the Receiver from going into a trance (or realizing the active imagination scene). Once the Receiver closes his eyes, the Pitcher is to use constructive verbal technique, but incongruent gestures. For example, if the Pitcher is talking about going down a staircase, she can use a progressively higher tone of voice. If the Pitcher is asking the Receiver to slow down his breathing, she can subtly speed up the tempo of her suggestions, etc. It is important to be subtle in using incongruence.

Once the exercise is completed, participants should discuss the experience.

Variations:

1. The Pitcher chooses a specific technique to accomplish the blocking task, e.g., being preoccupied or self-absorbed, being forgetful, withholding, being overly reassuring, providing unneeded approval, indiscriminately disagreeing, excessively probing, being challenging, or giving too much advice. The Receiver is not told that blocking will be part of the exercise. It is best to choose one specific style of blocking. The Pitcher should stay consistent, and increase the amount and/or intensity of gradually blocking during the course of induction.
2. The Pitcher identifies the primary communication blocking strategy of his mother, and blocks similarly. The exercise is then repeated by identifying and using his father's blocking strategy.
3. The Pitcher performs one induction and takes two roles: blocking from one position, e.g., of the father when leaning to the right; and blocking from the position of the mother when leaning to the left.
4. When out of the room, the Receiver is secretly instructed to make a subtle action, such as lightly tapping his fingers or smiling awkwardly, whenever he feels uncomfortable during the exercise.

Purpose: To realize the power of paraverbal communication.

Discussion: Warm-up Exercise 10

Clinicians can learn that small incidents of incongruence may affect outcomes. It is especially important for therapists to congruently coordinate verbal and nonverbal messages.

If participants can identify ways of blocking communication, they can also identify ways of avoiding (and even dealing with) blocking maneuvers. This exercise is similar to Warm-up Exercise 1, but it is more subtle.

SUMMARY AND DISCUSSION: WARM-UP EXERCISES

Let's return to the concept that being a therapist is a state, not a social role. The Warm-up Exercises elicit states and concepts that can enhance therapy. They also prime states needed for the Psychoaerobic Exercises that follow. The Warm-up Exercises elicit states that can be useful to therapists of any persuasion, and with any level of experience. It is a goal of this program to teach from the bottom up, experientially, rather than the top down, cognitively.

As a product of graduate school education, aspiring therapists become avid listeners. They learn to be empathic, inquisitive, supportive, accepting, genuine, and educational. These skills are taught didactically (top down), whereas constructive therapist states can be elicited bottom-up, through experiential exercises.

Here is a list of states and concepts that can be valuable in clinical work and coaching:

- Tolerate incompetence.
- Be playful.
- Develop the state of "being experiential." Change can be lived in the moment.
- Create empathy experientially. Access and utilize resonance.
- Have expressive emotional range.
- Develop implicit assessment of emotions.
- Use analogies, metaphors, and symbols.
- Improve somatic awareness. Use the body to communicate, for example, with gestures and postures.
- Be creative.
- Change states fluidly.
- Make minimal strategic changes that have a cumulative effect.
- Understand and utilize contextual and systemic effects.
- Build on the positive.
- Realize the importance of gesture and expression in empowering (or disempowering) a message.

This is the list of experiential goals that underlie the Warm-up Exercises. My procedure to develop the exercises was as follows: First, identify a globally encompassing state or concept; in this case, "good therapist." Then, create experiential exercises that help the communicator access elements of the global state or concept.

Whether or not the reader agrees with my list of states, or the generic characteristics of effective therapist states, is of secondary importance. Of primary importance is the experiential procedure.

The list of 14 concepts/states subdivides the global concept of "therapist" into components. In this model, "therapist" is considered a state. In a context called therapy, one of the participants accesses a number of the 14 components to become therapist. It is not necessary to access all of them, just a sufficient number to elicit the state of therapist. "Therapist" can be elicited from the bottom up by redintegrating partial cues.

The underlying heuristic of this model is: *Don't treat categories; address components.* Therapist is a category. Therapist can be elicited from the bottom up by activating components. The model can also be applied to problems. Take, for example, the problem of depression. Depression is a category. A psychiatrist's medical diagnosis of depression in a patient most often leads to a treatment plan using pharmaceuticals. Diagnosing depression, according to traditional psychiatric nomenclature, helps the psychiatrist decide on the proper medical treatment according to the professionally understood standard of care.

Non-psychiatric practitioners may take a different tact, and use social construction rather than medical diagnosis for assessment. From the perspective of social construction, depression can be considered a title for a number of component substates. Dividing depression into substates creates opportunities for systemic and social interventions. Depression can be considered a system composed of elements, including thoughts, feelings, behaviors, attitudes, perceptions, sensations, memories, and relationship patterns. A phenomenological map of depression can be created, and each of the elements can be considered an ineffective substate. The States Table can be used to create a "map" of the problem state.

A person could classify his experience as depression because he has: bad thoughts, sad feelings, impaired ability for action, self-loathing, internally focused perceptions, lethargy, haunting memories, and/or social withdrawal. Having this map in hand, a clinician can create situations that lead to constructive experiential realizations. It would not be necessary to address all the components because depression is a system, and modifying one or more components can have a systemic effect. The principle is: *Make the minimal number of changes that alter the system.* A corollary principle is to work in from the periphery. Start with components that are secondary to the client, and thereby more amenable to change. Central components are often recalcitrant, more resistant to change. Once a sufficient number of components are altered, even if they are peripheral, the client can "spontaneously" change the ineffective state.

For example, if self-loathing seems central to a person's depression, perhaps it would be best to initially address internally focused perceptions. This goal could be initiated within the session or with a homework assignment using an awareness exercise. For example, Dr. Erickson effectively assigned a task to a depressed woman who was an artist. She was to look for "a flash of color." A child on a bicycle was a flash of color; a bird flying overhead was a flash of color; so were the tree limbs and leaves blowing in the wind. She played the find a flash-of-color game with her children, and Dr. Erickson reported that the intervention was helpful in developing a brighter disposition.

Simply stated, one can subdivide a state, and perhaps the divisions are decided arbitrarily. A role, such as being a therapist, can be considered a state, because by doing so it may be easier to create divisions that can be experientially accessed. Problems such as depression can be divided into component states that can be addressed strategically and experientially. Goals, such as happiness, can be treated similarly. Happiness is the title for a state composed of components. I even apply this model to hypnotic induction. I view hypnosis as an amalgamation of elements, and not as a singularity. In composing an induction, I set into motion a number of concepts and substates, inviting the client to play with those elements. As the client stimulates the elements into play, hypnosis is created. An induction does not create hypnosis; eliciting elements allows the client to access the category. (For more information see Zeig, 2014.)

An apt metaphor for the Psychoaerobic system would be the specialized stations at fitness gyms designed to work certain muscle groups. One station isolates biceps; another isolates triceps. Overall physical fitness is developed by isolating and exercising body components. In the process of achieving the ideal physical state, one might discover a relative weakness in one component. Perhaps the biceps are more hypertrophied than the triceps. To correct the disparity, more exercises can be done that promote growth in the triceps.

Similarly, for some students, specific Warm-up Exercises will be easy and others will be difficult. The ones that are difficult may be practiced repeatedly to foster strength in those areas.

Now that the Psychoaerobics system has been outlined, the next section will focus on Milton Erickson. Again, modeling will be used. We will examine Erickson closely, paying special attention to the concepts and states that he developed during his career. Experiential exercises are proposed to access and develop those states.

SECTION III
Psychoaerobic Exercises

"All truly wise thoughts have been thought already thousands of times; but to make them truly ours, we must think them over again honestly, till they take root in our personal experience."

—Goethe

PSYCHOAEROBIC EXERCISES 1 & 2
An Introduction

There is an anecdote, the authenticity of which lies somewhere between fact and fiction, about Dr. Erickson and one of his adolescent sons. One afternoon, the son approached his father with a series of interesting, yet seemingly unrelated stories. One story may have been about a family outing, and another, about a vacation. A third story concerned his son's visit with his grandparents. Dr. Erickson found the stories amusing, but before his son could finish the third story, Dr. Erickson interrupted, "No, I'm sorry, you cannot borrow the car." He then gently coached his son in art of storytelling, explaining that when his son told the stories, he was unnecessarily direct both when mentioning the car keys, and when he talked about taking the car on a drive.

I suspect that growing up in the Erickson home was quite different than being raised in a traditional household. And I commend his son on tailoring a message to suit Dr. Erickson's anecdotal style. His son, moreover, was practicing *orienting toward*—a state central to Dr. Erickson's approach.

The literature regarding Dr. Erickson's methods touts him as being indirect. But, he was orienting toward, which is best conceived as a state, a way of being in the world. Derived from the state of orienting toward, indirection is a series of techniques, including the use of anecdotes and strategic language forms, including truisms and presuppositions. (For information on the language of hypnosis, see Zeig, 2014.) Note that the state is the progenitor of the technique. Orienting toward is a state. Indirection is a class of methods. Dr. Erickson created many techniques during his career, most of which were born from his state of orienting toward.

To shed light on the concept of orienting toward, consider the bilevel nature of communication. Every message has meaning on both a social and a psychological level (Berne, 1972). Communication is both informative and evocative. An example is flirting. Consider the evocative meaning when a man says to his date, "Want to come up to my apartment and see my etchings?" Clearly, information about art is not the target. Since humans are experts at bi-level communication, the receiver often seamlessly responds to the latent content, which is inferential. Human protolanguage and the communication strategies of animals are based on propositional meaning. Symbolic, verbal language cannot escape its roots.

Human communication is simultaneously informational and evocative. Scientists strive to communicate by providing facts, but concepts may be imbedded and transmitted. Although artists make concepts center stage, facts form the backdrop.

In the hypnosis literature, there has been needless controversy about the efficacy of direct versus indirect suggestions. Some messages are most effective when they're presented directly, as for example, education in the sciences. Other communications are best presented by orienting toward. The taproot of artistic expression is implication. Artists use conceptual methods such as abstraction, metaphor, and destabilization to orient toward. Musicians do not explain to listeners what they should feel. Painters do not tell viewers how to understand their art. Poets do not footnote their metaphors. Directors and do not explain to viewers the plot of the movie they are about to see. Rather, they strategically place hints in the movie using a propositional mechanism known as "setup and payoff."

A classic setup/payoff technique in film is to create an allusion to the plot during the title treatment, or early on in the movie. Those who have seen *The Wizard of Oz* have experienced the orienting-toward method. In the opening scene, Dorothy encounters three farmhands, plus the busybody who captures her dog, and an itinerant huckster. Hence, we are privy to the eccentricities of the personalities of the Scarecrow, the Tin Man, the Lion, the Wicked Witch, and the Wizard, when they are presented and exaggerated in Dorothy's fantasy. The setup-and-payoff technique of orienting toward have the intended effect: The viewer energizes the target concepts, which are elicited, not informed. Direct, overt methods would not evoke the desired response.

I am using art as an explanatory device with strategic intent. Most of us have developed media literacy and artistic literacy as a byproduct of social living. Our biological, evolutionary design is to intuitively grasp art, which has inference as a foundation.

The arts are evocative, not informative. When the goal of the communication is to elicit concepts and states rather than to provide facts, artistic methods of orienting toward should be harnessed. Using artistic methods to communicate is nothing new or strange. We are familiar with these methods. Evocative, conceptual communication is a matter of using what you already know: Take methods from one field and apply them strategically in another. Take orientations from art and use them conversationally when you want to elicit emotional impact.

Psychoaerobic Exercises 1 and 2 are designed to elicit two fundamental states: orienting toward (a form of gift-wrapping) and resonance (a form of "gift *un*wrapping"). The Pitcher explores the orienting-toward state; the Receiver, the state of resonance. Rather than cognitively attempting to understand the subtext of the Pitcher's method, the Receiver allows his body to resonate with the Pitcher's expression. Warm-up Exercise 3 was designed for practice in being resonant, in preparation for Psychoaerobic Exercises 1 and 2. Remember the metaphor of tuning forks? The Pitcher sets up a vibration, and like a similarly pitched tuning fork, the Receiver allows a response to "just happen." Resonance is a state of implicit responsiveness to the propositional meaning of the communication.

In order to best accomplish the goal states for each of the participants, restrictions are put in place. Strengths are eliminated so that previously underused resources can be stimulated into play. The technique is similar to the treatment of a child's amblyopia, or a stroke patient's deficits. The strengths are restricted so that the inferior function can be developed. The child's good eye is patched so that the deficient one grows stronger; the stroke patient's functional limb is restricted so that the nonfunctioning limb will gain strength and coordination. Similarly, in the next exercises, the Pitcher is limited to speaking in monotone without the use of gesture, so that the essentials of orienting toward can be realized. Even with these restrictions, the implied message can stimulate a response in the Receiver. The Receiver is restricted from responding verbally in order to maximize the possibility of experiencing resonance.

Psychoaerobic Exercises 1 and 2 are foundational for creating some of the more advanced forms of evocative therapeutic communication that Dr. Erickson used, including the therapeutic use of storytelling, metaphor, and the interspersal technique. (Erickson, 1964/2008a)

EXPERIENTIAL EMPOWERMENT
PSYCHOAEROBIC$_{SM}$ Exercises
www.psychoaerobic.org

PSYCHOAEROBIC EXERCISE 1

Clinician Posture to Develop: Orienting Toward and Resonance

Format: Dyads. Paper and pencil for the Receiver.

Roles: Receiver and Pitcher. It is best if the Pitcher and Receiver do not know each other. Roles need not be exchanged; they will be reversed in Exercise 2.

Method: The Receiver asks the Pitcher five simple questions, to which the Pitcher can answer "yes," "no," or "sometimes." An example: "Do you enjoy action movies?" The questions should not have obvious answers such as, "Are you female?" Writing down all questions before beginning the exercise is recommended for two reasons: The exercise will flow more smoothly, and the focus on the goal states will be better maintained.

The Pitcher (the person in the orienting-toward state) must answer the presented question in a restricted way. The Pitcher will speak in a slow, measured monotone using a "hypnotic" voice, and tell a brief story (three-minute maximum) that *means* "yes," "no," or "sometimes." The story need not be profound or complex. The subject of the story can be simple and commonplace. For example, she might talk about breakfast. The subject of the story should *not* allude in any way to the intent of the message, which is to communicate "yes," "no," or "sometimes" (the psychological-level message). If the subject of the story is too flowery or too dark, the Receiver will use the content to cognitively ascertain the implicit message. The Pitcher is to keep her face and body still when telling the story, to avoid offering cues through expressions or gestures.

The Receiver (the person in the resonant state) is a passive recipient. He can look at the Pitcher with a "soft focus," accessing the state of resonance, or gift unwrapping. The Receiver allows his *body* to respond as much as possible, turning off his analytic left hemisphere.

The Pitcher must watch the Receiver carefully when telling the story. The Pitcher should attend to the Receiver's physical clues—does his head subtly nod or shake during the story? Does the Receiver move forward or shy away? The Pitcher should continue the story until she a notices significant physical responses from the Receiver. When there are noticeable responses that seem to indicate, "yes," "no," or "sometimes," the Pitcher can stop the story and ask the Receiver for the next question. It is not important to get the "right" response—this comes with practice. More important is noticing *any* overt sign that appears to be a response to the psychological-level message.

It is helpful if the group leader first demonstrates the exercises.

After the exercise, the Pitcher describes the orienting-toward state she experienced, even if it was momentary, and the Receiver defines the "gift unwrapping" state, the state of resonance. The States Table (pp) can be used. It is advisable to have one or two core phenomenological descriptions that can be used in the future to access the orienting-toward state when it is desirable to do so. For example, the Pitcher could say: "I know I was in the orienting-toward state because I was visually focused." The Receiver and Pitcher can provide feedback to each other to further consolidate markers of the state, e.g., the Receiver can offer: "When you were orienting toward, you slowed down you speech." Pitcher: "When you were in your gift unwrapping state, you turned your head slightly to the left."

Discerning the "correct" meaning of the story is not the point of the exercise. The goal is to define the state, not to be immediately competent at eliciting responses to psychological level messages.

Variations:

1. The story is told subvocally, in gibberish, or using just one syllable, e.g., "bah" or "duh." In each case, the story should be told as if the speaker were using words and gestures in a normal way. Exaggerated pantomime should be avoided.
2. The Receiver asks a question and then closes his eyes and attends to the story so that the Pitcher can use gestures and expression.
3. The same story is told twice to respond to two separate questions – once to indicate "yes," and once to indicate "no."
4. The participants reverse roles and repeat the exercise (but it is

preferable to do Exercise 2 first).

Purpose: The Receiver must define phenomenologically what it is like to extract meaning (i.e., entering the state of resonance). The Pitcher must define phenomenologically what it is like to compose and deliver an implicit message (i.e., entering the "orienting-toward" state of delivering a psychological-level message).

Note: As with any experiential exercise, participation is voluntary.

EXPERIENTIAL EMPOWERMENT
PSYCHOAEROBIC$_{SM}$ Exercises
www.psychoaerobic.org

PSYCHOAEROBIC EXERCISE 2

Clinician Posture to Develop: Orienting Toward; Resonance.

Format: Dyads.

Roles: Participants use the same partners as in Exercise 1, but reverse roles.

Method: There are two conditions: condition A and condition B. Condition A will consist of negative emotions/states. Condition B will be positive emotions/states. In total, there will be four descriptions: two for Condition A (negative emotions), and two for condition B (positive emotions). The Pitcher's presentation order should be varied so that the Receiver will not know if the presented description is positive or negative.

Condition A: The Pitcher describes an object, first telling the Receiver the name of the object. Perhaps the Pitcher describes a tennis racket. But in her description, the Pitcher implicitly communicates a negative state or emotion, e.g., rage, anger, hostility, sadness, hurt, fear, guilt, embarrassment, grief, loneliness, confusion, loneliness, vulnerability, shyness, or depression. The Pitcher can describe the object in minute detail and implicitly build slowly and progressively toward the target emotion while monitoring the Receiver's state of resonance. In the second iteration, the same (or a new) object is used, but a different negative emotion/state is targeted.

Condition B: The Pitcher describes a different object, perhaps a glass of water, and communicates a positive emotion or state, e.g., awe, passion, love, affection, admiration, pride, self-respect, excitement, interest, relief, peacefulness, confidence, happiness, trust, hope, motivation, or positive expectation. In the second iteration, the same (or a new) object is used, but a different positive emotion is targeted.

Similar to Exercise 1, descriptions by the Pitcher should be made in slow, measured tones, using a "hypnotic" voice, while maintaining eye contact with the Receiver. The Pitcher should restrict gestures and expression, gradually stimulating the experience of the target emotion in the Receiver using inference. The Pitcher can stop the description when she notices behavioral evidence that the target emotion has been accessed. For example, there may be minute changes around the eyes or mouth that are micro-expressions of emotions/states.

The Receiver should resonate, and allow his body to experience the emotion being "pitched." To help do this, the Receiver can maintain a soft focus.

After the exercise, the Pitcher and Receiver discuss the phenomenology of what it was like respectively to orient toward, and to resonate with the implied message. Each provides helpful feedback about what the other looked like when he/she was most effective at being in the orienting-toward or gift unwrapping states. Core phenomenological anchors can be identified for accessing the state so it can be accessed as needed in the future.

Variations:

1. The Receiver can be asked to leave the room so that instructions can be given privately to the Pitcher. The Receiver would not be told that the latent content of the description will be an emotion.
2. The Receiver closes his eyes during the description, at which time the Pitcher can use physical mannerisms and gestures, but vocal expression should be restricted.
3. The Pitcher describes the same object, e.g., a tennis racquet, and conveys a positive emotion in the first iteration and a negative emotion in the second.
4. Participants reverse roles and repeat the exercise (assuming they have first completed Exercise 1).

Homework: When having lunch with a friend, try to elicit a target emotion by subtly using gestures, postures, or voice tone variations.

Purpose: The Receiver phenomenologically defines what it is like to elicit meaning (i.e., enter the "gift unwrapping" state of resonance). The Pitcher phenomenologically defines what it is like to compose and deliver an implicit message (i.e., entering the "orienting-toward" state of offering a psychological-level message.)

Discussion: Psychoaerobic Exercises 1 and 2

Consider the difference between Exercise 1 and Exercise 2. In the first exercise, the Pitcher orients to a thought. In the second exercise, the Pitcher orients to a feeling. These two elements of orienting toward form the foundation of one of Dr. Erickson's most ingenious methods: the interspersal technique (Erickson, 1966/2008a). The interspersal technique is an associative method. In contradistinction, the confusion technique (Erickson, 1964/2008b), another of Dr. Erickson's central contributions, was a dissociative technique. Associative and dissociative techniques can be used in tandem, similar to how consonance and dissonance are used in music composition.

The interspersal technique was introduced in one of Dr. Erickson's most famous cases: Joe and the Tomato Plant. Joe, a florist, had terminal cancer and none of the available treatments were effective in helping him manage his pain. Dr. Erickson was called to the hospital for a consult. A selection from Dr. Erickson's transcript follows: (Note: Italics are used to denote interspersed hypnotic suggestions uttered with a slightly different intonation.)

> ...I'm going to say a lot of things to you, but it won't be about flowers because you know more than I do about flowers. That isn't what you want. Now as I talk, and I can do so *comfortably*, I wish that you will *listen to me comfortably* as I talk about a tomato plant. That is an odd thing to talk about. It makes one *curious. Why talk about a tomato plant?* One puts a tomato seed in the ground. One can *feel hope* that it will grow into a tomato plant that *will bring satisfaction* by the fruit it has. The seed soaks up the water. *Not very much difficulty* in doing that because of the rain that *brings peace and comfort...* And *you can listen to me,* Joe, so I will keep on talking and *you can keep on listening, wondering, just wondering what you can really learn...* (pp. 105)

In this particular case, Dr. Erickson described an object. On the social level, he talked about a tomato plant. On the psychological level, he interspersed therapeutic suggestions. From my personal experience with Dr. Erickson, I would posit that the therapeutic concepts in italics might have been spoken using under emphasis, which is a softer, subtler way of making interspersed ideas stand out as signal. Therefore, the noise, the surface concept (talking about tomato plants), would recede into the background. The concepts in italics also might have been signaled by a subtle shift in tempo or direction of his voice.

Dr. Erickson was using parallel communication. Of course, discussion of the tomato plant was not the point of the conversation. The therapeutic message (in this case, the modification of pain) was presented in a parallel. He was orienting Joe to memories and ideas that would set in motion a train of associations to modify the experience of pain, as Joe mentally activated to find personal meaning in Dr. Erickson's message.

Hypnotic inductions are commonly created by using psychological-level communication. On a social level the hypnotist might talk about walking on the beach, but on a psychological level he would mean: You can alter your attention; modify the intensity of your experience, dissociate, and respond to the meaning of my communication. (For information about hypnotic induction see Zeig, 2014.) Again, induction does not create hypnosis. Orienting-toward components elicits trance.

The use of metaphor in hypnotic or non-hypnotic psychotherapy operates similarly to the interspersal method. The metaphor is a parallel, a context for talking to the patient about how to cope with, or surmount, the problem. Perhaps the therapist talks on the surface level about walking on a mountain path and meeting a wise woman who offers advice. The subtext and embedded messages in the metaphor orients the patient in therapeutic directions.

Psychoaerobic Exercises 1 and 2 are designed to help students develop states that are fundamental to hypnotic induction and the use of psychological-level methods as treatment tools in psychotherapy. Again, these exercises need to be practiced repeatedly to develop the intended states of orienting toward. In effecting psychotherapy, clinicians can orient to a thought, to a feeling, to a behavior, etc. The summative effect is to elicit constructive associations that empower adaptive change in concepts, states, and identity. The power of implication can be harnessed therapeutically.

I find it curious that Milton Erickson was the first therapist to demonstrate the value of psychological-level communication as a treatment tool. In fact, he built his practice of hypnosis and psychotherapy around the propositional meaning that underlies communication. Remember that he was a social psychologist before the field of social psychology was widely recognized as a distinct science. Social psychology studies effects, such as priming, social mimicry, attributions, demand characteristics, emotional contagion, inattentional blindness, and obedience to authority. All of these effects are based on how people respond on the psychological level, without necessarily realizing their response or the cue that precipitated the response.

I do not believe Dr. Erickson thought beforehand about the mechanics of indirection, although *ex post facto*, he could describe his moment to moment intent. Rather, I believe that he developed the state of orienting toward in his procedural memory. From that state, techniques would follow, and the result would be indirect suggestions, metaphor, and the interspersal technique.

"The real act of discovery consists not in finding new lands,
but in seeing with new eyes."

—Marcel Proust

PSYCHOAEROBIC EXERCISE 3-12
An Introduction

Psychoaerobic Exercises 3-12 introduce a new therapeutic state. Allow me to preface the section with a story. Perhaps this story is just that, an unsubstantiated story; nonetheless its theme is useful in providing an introduction to the state to be developed in the next exercises.

Dr. Erickson is known as one of history's most perceptive clinicians. The stories about his ability to discern and effectively utilize nuances in patient behavior are legendary. The anthropologist, Raymond Birdwhistell, invented the field of Kinesics, which is the study of physical movements and expressions and their nonverbal implications. Birdwhistell approached nonverbal behavior from a research perspective, and his perceptiveness was also legendary.

In the 1960s, when Erickson was lecturing in Philadelphia, Erickson and Birdwhistell met at Birdwhistell's home. During the visit, Dr. Erickson saw a carving that he coveted, so he was careful not to offer any discernible cues. As Dr. Erickson was leaving, Birdwhistell thanked him for the visit and said, "And of course you can have the carving." Even though Dr. Erickson tried to mask his admiration of the carving, there were enough cues for an observer of Birdwhistell's stature to discern Erickson's sentiments.

Although it would be daunting to match the perceptiveness of these two men, it is possible for all of us to improve. The question is: How do we go about it? In talking about seeing new patients, Dr. Erickson said, "I would turn on my gaze." Using the states model, it seems that Dr. Erickson entered a state of acuity, which is the subject of the next exercises.

Some people say you can't have enough love; others say you can't have enough money. As far as psychotherapy is concerned, you can't have enough acuity. Acuity is something that can be developed over the course of a lifetime, and practicing acuity exercises can promote neurogenesis of "acuity" regions of the brain. Improving discernment can be valuable in all aspects of life. To begin, it is important to understand that acuity is not a singularity.

Acuity is a construct of convenience; it's a title that people use to simplify communication. To improve acutity, it is important to understand component substates. The following exercises are designed to foster acuity substates. Return to the model of strength training in a gym. Each station is designed to isolate certain muscle groups so that they can be hypertrophied. Depending on your customary daily activities and previous sessions of physical exercise, different muscles will start off stronger than others. Based upon your genetic make-up, some muscles will be easier to advance because they naturally have a higher potential. To achieve overall fitness, spend more time exercising inferior functions and monitor your progress. Similarly, there can be a number of "stations" for building components of acuity.

Exercise 3 contains a number of component dimensions. It requires readers to focus on specific sections of the handout. After you read the handout and experience each section, a description of the intended components follows. To get the most out of the experience, take time with each section, and consider the state that it is designed to help you develop. Exercise 3 is to be done privately, but using group dynamics in the discussion period can make it more effective.

EXPERIENTIAL EMPOWERMENT
PSYCHOAEROBIC$_{SM}$ Exercises
www.psychoaerobic.org

PSYCHOAEROBIC EXERCISE 3

Clinician Posture to Develop: Acuity: Realizing the psychological determinants of perception.

Format: Handout.

Roles: Each participant works independently.

Method: The observers read the words below as instructed by the group leader.

Hithere.
Loveisnowhere.
Theytoldhimtobeatthefrontdoor.
DOCTOR RAKES LEAVES AFTER MEETING.
Would you rather have an elephant eat you or a gorilla?
Woman without her man would be nothing.

How many times does the letter "F" appear in the following sentence?

Finished files are the result of years of scientific study combined with the experience of many years.

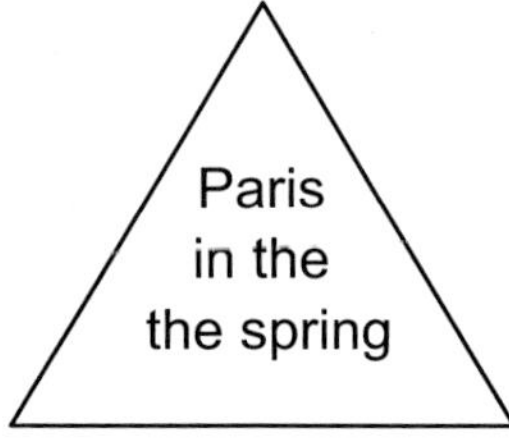

The sentence below is printed backward. Read the sentence once from right to left.

".rat eht saw tac ehT"

Read the following sentence six times, extracting a different meaning with each repetition.

I never said he stole money.

Discussion: Psychoaerobic Exercise 3

The first section consists of six sentences that are examples of ambiguity. The first three sentences can be read two different ways—one, more affectionately, and the other, more aggressively. For example, the first sentence could be read "hi there" or "hit here."

The fourth sentence, that begins with "DOCTOR RAKES..." is a distinct type of ambiguity. It depends on whether you perceive RAKES as a proper noun (name) or a verb. The fifth sentence can also be understood in two different ways. Take time to discover both meanings.

The sixth sentence is an ambiguous statement about gender roles. The meaning of the sentence depends on where one pauses when saying it.

It is easy to misread the backward sentence below the triangle. Our need to have things make sense according to our understanding of the world is such that we may distort reality to conform to our preconceptions. There is no reason to believe from the outset that that sentence will be meaningful, but because sentences usually are meaningful, we may distort what is written to derive rational meaning.

Several examples of distorting reality in the field of psychotherapy come to mind. Our perceptions are influenced by favored theoretical constructs. For instance, when I studied transactional analysis and became a Clinical Member, TA theories led me to recognize ego states, rackets, existential positions, games, and scripts. When I studied Gestalt therapy, I focused on projections; when I studied psychodynamic psychotherapy, I saw transference. Every school of therapy imprints a lens in the eyes of aficionados—one that both focuses and distorts.

The last sentence on the page—"I never said he stole money"—can be read six different ways, depending on how one distinctively emphasizes each word. Small changes can lead to different meanings.

I usually begin Exercise 3 by asking students to silently read the words written in the triangle. I focus on a student, who when queried, identifies himself as reading "Paris in the spring." I ask that student to stand up so that other members of the group can focus on him. I explain that it does not say, "Paris in the spring." I ask the student to read the words aloud one by one until he realizes what it actually says – "Paris in the the spring," suddenly, the student has an "Aha!" experience. I explain that "Aha!" moments are the result of experiential techniques. They empower change in therapy...and in life.

Next, I may ask students to look at the rectangle and silently count the number of times the letter "F" appears. I may ask a student who reports seeing the letter "F" three times to stand up and recite all letters in the sentence, to further exemplify the "Aha!" moment. Both the triangle and rectangle graphics demonstrate the brain's tendency to ignore redundancy. The brain is a mismatch detector, designed to notice aberrations in any given situation. In a stationary field, one notices movement; things that don't move may not be fully registered in perception. In a lineup of tall people, the one short person is quickly noticed, and the tall people may be ignored. Part of our evolutionary biology is to perceptually delete steady-state information. The brain minimizes energy by ignoring things that do not seem immediately compelling. For example, the sound of a car engine is most often ignored because it is redundant. Therapists, however, should attend to redundancies, because they are often skeleton keys that open constructive doors.

I have used Exercise 3 with patients to help them realize concepts. For example, if denial is part of the problem, I might ask a patient to view the triangle and rectangle. I want the patient *to get* the concept of overlooking the obvious. Again, my design is to create the dots, not connect them.

In this simple exercise there are four substates of acuity:

1. Attending to redundancy.

2. Appreciating (and using) ambiguity.

3. Having a beginner's mind. Seeing what is there, even if it doesn't conform to preconceptions.

4. Seeing that small variations can alter meaning.

The next exercise is interactive, and addresses another substate: visual acuity to detail.

EXPERIENTIAL EMPOWERMENT
PSYCHOAEROBIC$_{SM}$ Exercises
www.psychoaerobic.org

PSYCHOAEROBIC EXERCISE 4

Clinician Posture to Develop: Visual acuity to detail.

Format: Dyads.

Roles: One Pitcher; one Receiver.

Method: The Pitcher and Receiver sit or stand face-to-face. The Receiver accesses an acuity state, studiously examining and "memorizing" the Pitcher. The Receiver closes her eyes. Then, the Pitcher makes three physical changes, perhaps turning his collar up, taking off his belt, and messing up his hair. The Pitcher tells the Receiver to open her eyes and identify the three changes.

The Receivers are instructed by the group leader: "Let your eyes discover the changes. They may do so even before you think about the changes. Trust what your eyes guide you to see. They may unconsciously guide you to the changes."

The Receiver is to identify the "state" of "turning on your gaze." If one's sole focus is being right, it may interfere with identifying and developing the intended state. This exercise is not a competition.

The Pitchers and Receivers reverse roles.

Variations:

1. Both players turn away and make changes simultaneously.
2. After the exercise is done once, the members of the dyad find new partners and repeat the exercise.
3. The Pitcher makes three changes in posture and gesture.
4. The Pitcher makes three changes in the immediate environment.

Purpose: The Receiver must identify experientially what it is like to attend to visual details, i.e., the specifics of the acuity state. "Specifically, how do you *know* that you were in the 'turning on your gaze' state?" Think about how you can use those anchors to access that state when needed.

Application: With disengaged couples or families. Use when couples or families are not "seeing" each other, etc. For team building and/or breaking the ice when offering organizational development training.

Adapted from Viola Spolin's *Improvisation for the Theater,* and Kipling's *The Jungle Book.*

Discussion: Psychoaerobic Exercise 4

My daughter, Nicole, and I frequently played this game when she was younger. At a restaurant, I would ask her to close her eyes while I made three changes on the newly set table. (As we advanced, we would use a messy table, which would have fewer clues.) I would turn a glass upside down, remove a fork, and interchange cutlery. She would identify the changes. Then, I would close my eyes and she could make three changes. She would put a grain of salt on a plate, move a piece of silverware a millimeter, and put the slightest smudge on a water glass. Honing acuity became a challenge for both of us, but it was more daunting for me.

The purpose of Psychoaerobic Exercise 4 is to develop the state of visual attention to detail. Oftentimes, if unimpeded by conscious deliberation, free-flowing visual attention can be surprisingly accurate in making appraisals. Hence, I ask participants to trust their eyes and guess, based on where their eyes take them, rather than using conscious analysis. Their eyes may effectively use unconscious processing. When it comes to acuity, automatic behavior may be more intelligent than conscious reasoning.

As mentioned, there are many applications for Exercise 4. It can be modified for disengaged partners who are not "seeing" each other. The process of "seeing" can become a playful game that can empower couples to be more attentive to each other. It can be used in business training to promote more attentive employee relations and customer service.

Another substate of acuity—auditory and visual concentration—is presented in the next exercise.

EXPERIENTIAL EMPOWERMENT
PSYCHOAEROBIC$_{SM}$ Exercises
www.psychoaerobic.org

PSYCHOAEROBIC EXERCISE 5

Clinician Posture to Develop: Acuity: auditory and visual concentration.

Format: Group of six to eight sitting in a circle.

Method: One player begins with the sentence, "When I see my next client I will (add a descriptive word or simple phrase)." The second player repeats the entire sentence and *adds* an additional descriptive word or phrase. The third player repeats the sentence as stated by the second player, and adds another descriptive word or phrase. For example, "When I see my next client I will turn on my gaze, be more experiential, and focus my attention." Each player takes a turn adding a new concept. If a player does not say the expanding sentence exactly as stated, then that player is out. The game continues until only one player is left. Note: Before you begin, turn on your ears. Enter a state of auditory acuity.

Variations:

1. Conduct the exercise with eyes closed in order to focus on auditory concentration.
2. Add a related gesture with each added phrase. The subsequent player repeats the sentence and gesture, and then adds a new phrase and gesture.
3. Add an incongruent gesture—a gesture not related to the added concept, such as waving good-bye while saying, "I will drink more coffee."
4. Repeat the stimulus sentence, but add a gesture rather than a phrase, e.g., "When I see my next client I will respond by (add gestures successively)."

5. Add a sound rather than a descriptive phrase or gesture.
6. Sing the sentence rather than saying it. The next player mirrors the melody of the previous person and uses a new melody for the phrase he adds. Add a stanza on the end of the previous person's stanza.
7. Prior to the exercise, the leader provides generic strategies for participants to adopt: for example, the leader can offer a group trance to "turn on your eyes and ears, and enter the acuity state." The leader can suggest some mnemonic devices. He can instruct participants to mentally photograph each presented concept, tell them to listen especially to the last phrase spoken, and invite them to subtly mimic people as they say their phrase, etc.
8. Regardless of how well they do, participants describe their strategy to the group.
9. After the exercise, the group interviews the "experts," and tries to understand/model the expert's strategy/state by repeatedly asking questions, such as, "Specifically, how did you do that?" "What else did you do?" "What were you experiencing when you did that?" Then, the exercise is repeated, perhaps using one of the variations, and the group members adopt one of the experts' strategies/states. After the exercise, discuss the effects on each member of the group when they modeled and adopted an expert's strategy/state.

Purpose: To experientially develop the states of auditory and visual concentration, and attention.

Adapted from Viola Spolin, *Improvisation for the Theater.*

Discussion: Psychoaerobic Exercise 5

After the exercise, students are encouraged to reflect on the phenomenology of their states of visual and auditory concentration. This can be done privately, in discussion with another participant, or in the group.

When I conduct this exercise, I allow students to be liberal or strict when deciding whether or not the repetition is sufficiently accurate. Also, students are exhorted to do *their* best in order to discover their own abilities. The focus for group members is helping each other increase auditory and visual concentration. Competition should be absent, or at least minimized.

Most often, there are two iterations of this exercise. The first rendition uses only auditory prompts and the extended sentence is created solely by verbally adding phrases. For the second iteration, I ask the group to engage in the modeling process, and I use group hypnosis to provide suggestions that facilitate performance. Then, ask students to repeat the exercise and add visual concentration. Modeling and group hypnosis demonstrate to students that they can improve their concentration.

To accomplish modeling, I ask students to interview the experts in their group to discover a strategy/state that can be used in the next iteration. Students query the experts, asking, "Specifically, how did you do that?" This modeling question can be asked repeatedly. For example, if the expert says, "I visualized the added concept," the interviewers can further ask, "Specifically, how did you do that?" The interviewers also can repeatedly ask about the expert's state: "Specifically, what were you experiencing when you did that?" The modeling questions are asked to obtain the details of the expert's strategy/state so that the interviewer can find a strategy/state to use in the next iteration.

The second rendition uses new phrases and congruent gestures, such as, "When I see my next patient I will be more open (making an open gesture)," thereby adding visual concentration. The person who started in the first rendition must initiate the exercise. Again, prior to the second iteration, I offer a group induction designed to orient participants to further develop auditory and visual concentration, and to help participants experientially realize the strategy/state they have learned by interviewing the expert.

After the exercise, students are polled to ascertain improvement that has been fostered by the group hypnosis and adopted strategy/state. It is often the case that the performance of the experts decreases, whereas the performance of group members increases. Modeling may be the culprit. The strategies the expert uses, and the states the expert accesses in the first iteration, are a gestalt that is more than the sum of its parts. Making the expert conscious of the intricacies of his orientation can focus him on one aspect, thereby disturbing the gestalt. Overt modeling of an expert may not be good for the expert, but it can facilitate the performance of the modeler.

This exercise is valuable in many different realms because it is easy to follow and is engaging. It has many potential applications. The exercise can be adapted to serve as homework to promote cohesiveness in a family. It can foster team building in an organization. It can also be used to develop concentration in the classroom or in a psychotherapy supervision group.

When she was younger, my daughter and I would play this acuity exercise as a game using an alphabet version when we took long drives: "I did not go to school today because I had asthma." "I did not go to school today because I had asthma and bronchitis." "I did not go to school today because I had asthma, bronchitis, and a cold," etc. Often she had to prompt me so that I could keep up the game.

EXPERIENTIAL EMPOWERMENT
PSYCHOAEROBIC$_{SM}$ Exercises
www.psychoaerobic.org

PSYCHOAEROBIC EXERCISE 6

Clinician Posture to Develop: Visual and auditory acuity to patterns.

Format: Group fishbowl (One participant who becomes the Pitcher sits in front of the group).

Roles: A person from the group is selected to be the Pitcher. If possible, the Pitcher should be a native speaker of a foreign language that is not familiar to members of the group. Other group members are Receivers.

Method: Speaking in his native language, the Pitcher tells two sets of stories. Each story should be short, approximately five to 10 sentences in length. One of the stories must contain an emotionally significant lie. The lie cannot be a simple factual distortion. The other story must be entirely true. After each pair of stories, students vote with a show of hands, indicating which story is true and which is false. The Pitcher then indicates which story contained the lie. The Pitcher will need to present several sets of stories. After three or four pairs of stories, the Pitcher leaves the room. The group is polled to determine the experts in lie detection. The experts are asked to describe their successful states/strategies. Subsequently, the Pitcher is asked to return to the room and tell another set (or two) of stories. The students can adopt the strategies of the experts. When the exercise is over, the group tells the Pitcher the pattern he used when he was lying.

Acting as "human lie detectors," the Receivers notice subtle changes in behavior that could indicate the Pitcher is lying. When lying, perhaps gestures are asymmetric. Perhaps there are indicative eye movements. Perhaps posture is more restricted.

Remember: The goal is to define the acuity state for realizing patterns. Competency in lie detection can be developed by developing the acuity state of attending to patterns.

Variations:

1. The Receivers close their eyes and listen, determining the lie solely by using auditory cues.
2. The Receivers cover their ears tightly and watch as the story is being told, determining the lie by visual cues.
3. Half the group of Receivers close their eyes and listen, while the other half cover their ears and watch, in order to determine if visual or auditory clues are more effective.
4. As inducement for cleverly lying, the Pitcher is offered a reward for successfully deceiving the group.
6. The Pitcher tells three stories, rather than two, only one of which contains an emotionally significant lie.
7. The Pitcher tells the stories using gibberish, a single tone, or subvocal speech (using normal gestures and mouthing the words, but not actually speaking).
8. Prior to the exercise, the Pitcher initially tells a few simple lies to determine a possible pattern. Here is a possible procedure: The Pitcher is prompted to answer questions in ways that are obviously true and obviously false. For example, the Pitcher can be instructed to answer "Yes" and only "Yes" to some basic questions, such as, "Are you in this room?" "Are you wearing shoes?" "Do you own a phone?" Subsequently, some of the questions should be composed to prompt a lie. "Is your name is Ilsabeck?" "Are you in Turkestan now?" "Are you listening to classical music?" Perhaps a pattern will emerge that will help the lie detectors.

Purpose: Receivers identify the state of paying attention to visual and auditory patterns.

Discussion: Psychoaerobic Exercise 6

Poker players understand that other players often have what is known as a "tell," or a characteristic pattern when they are bluffing.

Poker experts are good at detecting lies. The strategies experts use can be learned and practiced, and will improve the game of any poker player.

The scientist, Paul Ekman, has assiduously researched the patterns of liars. Some of the characteristics of lying that he has discovered include asymmetric facial and gestural expressions, half gestures, and signs of increased peripheral arousal. (For more information, see *Telling Lies*, Ekman, 2009.) Oftentimes, when the Pitcher is out of the room, I tell students these cues to get them started.

To increase the amount of tension, Ekman paid experimental subjects for deceiving him. Increased tension can make detecting lies easier. When I conducted this exercise with groups, I have offered the Pitcher a free workshop or a free book for successful deception. This added incentive can decrease the person's ability to deceive the group.

It is best to conduct the exercise with a native speaker of a foreign language. This ensures that attention to content is minimized and attention to extra-verbal components is enhanced.

Remember, the purpose of the exercise is to improve the state of recognizing patterns. Discussion among group members should focus on identifying and enhancing that state.

EXPERIENTIAL EMPOWERMENT
PSYCHOAEROBIC$_{SM}$ Exercises
www.psychoaerobic.org

PSYCHOAEROBIC EXERCISE 7

Clinician Posture to Develop: Visual acuity to emotional response.

Format: Group. Pitcher and a Receiver sit in front of the group; the Pitcher has her back to the group and the Receiver faces the group.

Roles: Similar to Psychoaerobic Exercise 2, the Pitcher briefly describes an object, but in her description, the Pitcher implicitly communicates a specific positive or negative emotion. The description should gradually build toward the emotion. The Receiver silently resonates, experiencing the communicated emotion.

Method: Group members cover their ears to restrict hearing the Pitcher's description. The Pitcher chooses whether to present a positive or negative emotion. The group members enter an acuity state. By watching the expression of the Receiver, the group guesses whether the simulated emotion was positive or negative. The exercise is repeated with a different description and a different intended emotion.

Variations:

1. The exercise is repeated, but instead the Pitcher tells an emotional story.
2. The exercise is repeated, but the group is instructed to look between the Pitcher and Receiver, who sit facing each other so that the audience can observe the interaction. (The goal is to develop a state of understanding interaction patterns.)
3. The exercise is conducted in triads with one observer, rather than in a group.
4. The group members guess the projected emotion, instead of just

whether it was positive or negative.

5. The Pitcher tells the story subvocally, using gibberish, or a single tone.

Purpose: The observers identify and develop the "acuity state."

EXPERIENTIAL EMPOWERMENT
PSYCHOAEROBIC$_{SM}$ Exercises
www.psychoaerobic.org

PSYCHOAEROBIC EXERCISE 8

Clinician Posture to Develop: Visual and auditory acuity. Extrapolate meaning.

Format: Group. Two Pitchers—the discussants—sit in front of the group.

Roles: Two people who speak the same foreign language are identified as discussants. It is best if the language is uncommon so that the group does not understand.

If group members are not proficient in a foreign language, the Pitchers can speak gibberish, converse subvocally, or use just one syllable.

Method: The Pitchers secretly decide on a topic to discuss—the plot of a movie, planning a picnic, financial matters, etc. The Pitchers discuss a topic for three to five minutes using normal gestures at first, and then gradually to more openly express the meaning of the conversation.

The group identifies the topics discussed, the cues they discerned in order to make their guesses, and the specifics of their acuity state.

Purpose: The Receivers define and heighten their acuity state, and their ability to extrapolate meaning.

(Handout is given to participants after completing the exercise.)

EXPERIENTIAL EMPOWERMENT
PSYCHOAEROBIC$_{SM}$ Exercises
www.psychoaerobic.org

PSYCHOAEROBIC EXERCISE 9

Clinician Posture to Deveıop: Acuity to response.

Format: Dyads.

Roles: Pitchers and Receivers—in pairs.

Method: The Pitchers are told that they will be asked to tell a simple story of five or six sentences to the Receivers, who will then repeat the story back to them. The story can be about a common experience, such as driving to work. Then, the Pitchers are sent out of the room so that the leader can give instructions to the Receivers.

When the Pitchers finish the story, the Receivers are told to repeat the story as accurately as possible, adding to each sentence a modifier. For example, perhaps the Pitcher tells a story about going to the grocery store. The Receiver then repeats the story and adds, "I walked to the crowded store." "I bought healthy food." "I purchased Florida oranges." Again, one modifier is added to each sentence. The modifier can be random but should be minimal and not exaggerated.

When the Pitchers return, they tell the Receivers the story using five to six sentences. The Receivers access an acuity state.

As the Receivers modify the story, they attend to the response of the Pitchers. At the end of the exercise, the Receivers describe the Pitchers' behavioral responses to the modifications. The Receivers explain to the Pitchers the method used of adding modifiers to each sentence.

In the discussion period, the Receivers experientially define the acuity state and its phenomenological components.

Variations:

1. Receivers add a modifier and complementary gesture to each sentence.
2. Rather than adding a modifier, only add a gesture.
3. When repeating the story, the Receivers mirror the nonverbal communication used by the Pitchers, as much as possible.
4. All the modifiers used might be in the same category. For example, all could be sounds, feelings, sights, colors, etc.

Purpose: The Receivers strive to refine the acuity state.

Adapted from Viola Spolin, *Improvisation for the Theater.*
(Handout is given to participants after completing the exercise.)

EXPERIENTIAL EMPOWERMENT
PSYCHOAEROBIC$_{SM}$ Exercises
www.psychoaerobic.org

PSYCHOAEROBIC EXERCISE 10

Clinician Posture to Develop: Visual and auditory acuity to both interaction patterns and conspicuous absences.

Format: Pitcher and Receiver in front of the group; observers in the audience.

Method: The Pitcher and Receiver leave the room so that the group leader can secretly give them instructions. The Pitcher is directed to tell a story and make something conspicuously absent. Perhaps the Pitcher will not use adjectives, or he will not move his left hand, acting as if it is paralyzed. The Receiver is to interview the Pitcher. The Receiver is also programmed to nod, smile, and/or say "uh huh," whenever the Pitcher communicates a feeling. The observers are instructed to notice patterns. They are told the exercise is about acuity, but they are not told the categories of patterns to observe.

The Pitcher and Receiver return. The Pitcher tells his story and the Receiver interviews him about the story. After the story is completed the observers determine the patterns used by the Pitcher and Receiver.

Variations:

(Instructions for each variation can be given privately to the Pitcher and Receiver.)

1. The Pitcher paces his story so that he only speaks when the Receiver exhales.
2. The Pitcher nonverbally affirms the Receiver's smiles with a repeated gesture or expression.
3. The Receiver frowns and moves away whenever the Pitcher moves closer.

4. The Receiver does not maintain consistent eye contact with the Pitcher.
5. The Pitcher and Receiver synchronize their breathing rate, or mirror each other's facial expressions, etc.
6. The Receiver is programmed to use a repetitive phrase, such as, "I don't know, but...." The observers are to discover the redundancy.
7. Prior to the exercise, observers can be told to look *between* the Pitcher and Receiver (who are facing each other in front of the group) for an interaction pattern. They are also told that there will be a conspicuous absence in one of the partners.

Purpose: The observers describe the acuity states experienced while noticing interaction patterns and perceiving conspicuous absences.

Discussion: Psychoaerobic Exercise 10

The concept of "conspicuous absence" is an oxymoron, but one that is understandable. When training students, I advise them to note conspicuous absences in patients, whether individuals, couples, or families. There can be absences in any physical, psychological, or interpersonal sphere, including behavior, specific emotions, and interaction patterns. Not using modifiers or not finishing sentences are linguistic absences. Never smiling, gesturing, or making facial expressions when talking to another person are interpersonal absences.

Noticing conspicuous absences can be a surprisingly difficult task. However, it is a skill that can be developed through practice. It is possible that treatment can be facilitated by recognizing and understanding specific conspicuous absences in patients.

Becoming aware of interaction patterns can be difficult because it requires thinking in a "when-then" manner. For example, "When he does 'X,' then she does 'Y.'" It is uncommon to attend to interaction patterns, and we don't have adequate terms to describe them. Our vocabulary is designed to describe events that are intrapsychic, rather than interpersonal.

For example, if I asked for a definition of love, most would describe it intrapsychically, as a feeling of luminance, passion, admiration, caring, etc. But love is an interpersonal event. I made up the acronym, TOPIAH, as an interpersonal definition. It stands for Take Obvious Pleasure in Another's Happiness. It is the difference between a woman who comes home and is happy about the dinner her husband has prepared because she's hungry, and a woman who comes home and is happy for her husband because she knows cooking is his hobby and passion.

Once a therapist spends 100 hours in therapy with families, couples, or individuals, an understanding of interaction patterns may develop.

Variations of this exercise are endless. There are many classes of conspicuous absences and interaction patterns to observe. The focus of Exercise 10 is to expand the acuity state to include both the substates of noticing interaction patterns, and attending to conspicuous absences. Therapists of all persuasions can benefit from developing these substates.

Normally, I do not tell observers prior to the exercise the two categories of conspicuous absence and interaction patterns that will be used by the Pitcher and Receiver. I may tell them the two categories after the story has been told and prior to them guessing, so that they have a reference point for guessing.

EXPERIENTIAL EMPOWERMENT
PSYCHOAEROBIC$_{SM}$ Exercises
www.psychoaerobic.org

PSYCHOAEROBIC EXERCISE 11

Clinician Posture to Develop: To make predictions from minimal cues.

Format: Group.

Roles: None.

Method: Each person in the group reads the following passage, and then predicts what is said on the last page of the book. The passage is the opening page of *Nightmare Alley* by William Lindsay Gresham, Rinehart & Company, New York, © 1946.

Card I
The Fool
who walks in motley, with his
eyes closed, over a precipice
at the end of the world.

Stan Carlisle stood well back from the entrance of the canvas enclosure, under the blaze of a naked light bulb, and watched the geek.

This geek was a thin man who wore a suit of long underwear dyed chocolate brown. The wig was black and looked like a mop, and the brown greasepaint on the emaciated face was streaked and smeared with the heat and rubbed off around the mouth.

At present the geek was leaning against the wall of the pen, while around him a few—pathetically few— snakes lay in loose coils, feeling the hot summer night and sullenly uneasy in the glare. One slim little king snake was trying to climb up the wall of the enclosure and was falling back.

Stan liked snakes; the disgust he felt was for them, at their having to be penned up with such a specimen of man. Outside the talker was working up to his climax. Stan turned his neat blond head toward the entrance.

"...where did he come from? God only knows. He was found on an uninhabited island five hundred miles off the coast of Florida. My friends, in this enclosure you will see one of the unexplained mysteries of the universe. Is he man or is he beast? ..."

Purpose: To develop states of inference.

Discussion: Psychoaerobic Exercise 11

This exercise was one of several similar exercises that Dr. Erickson used early in my training. For example, he gave me an autobiography written by a patient. I was to read the first few paragraphs and then predict what was said at the end of the transcript. (This is recounted in my book, *Experiencing Erickson*, 1985.)

Dr. Erickson used the passage from *Nightmare Alley* similarly. He told me to read the first page of the book, and then predict what it would say on the last page. He said that his wife and one of his daughters read the book and enjoyed it. When they gave the book to him, he read the first page and predicted what it said on the last page. I did not have that talent. In Dr. Erickson's presence, I read the first page and fumbled. I had no idea what it said on the last page. When I asked him what it said, he told me to read the book. When I finished the book, I returned to the first page and reread it. It was clear that the author had seeded the end of his protagonist's story on the first page of the book. (Readers who are interested in learning more about the effective use of seeding in psychotherapy can find a chapter on the topic in my book, *Confluence,* 2006.)

There are many patterns in human behavior; some are composed of microdynamic (small) elements and some macrodynamic (large) elements. The founder of transactional analysis, Eric Berne, was an astute observer of processes in human behavior. One of his contributions to psychotherapy was his theory of psychological games, which are transactional sequences that are played out repeatedly in the service of experiencing a redundant bad feeling—for example, hurt or anger. He called this feeling a "racket." One of the games that Berne identified was named *Rapo*. The social version is: "Offer made. Offer accepted. Offer withdrawn (or acceptance withdrawn)." Or, "Offer or acceptance significantly modified after the fact." For example, one player would suggest a business arrangement. The other would agree, but then one of them would pull out, leaving the jilted player with a familiar bad feeling.

The rackety feelings advance what Berne called an *existential position* in the world. For instance, "I'm not okay; you're okay." In Berne's theory, a macrodynamic pattern is a *life script*, which could be considered the plot, or unconscious through-line that organizes one's life. Many folk stories are metaphors for life scripts, which could parallel the theme of a fairy tale, such as Cinderella or Snow White. The essential theme of Berne's work on games and life scripts was that *human behavior is unconsciously patterned and repetitive.* Understanding a microdynamic pattern (in this case, a game) could allow an observer to intuit a macrodynamic pattern (in this case, a life script).

Understanding redundancies in human behavior was important to Dr. Erickson. To help students develop the state of inference, he would suggest they read a good novel, beginning with the last chapter, and ending with the first chapter. He wanted students to predict what was written in each previous chapter before proceeding. Of course, the task could be accomplished by predicting the content of subsequent chapters.

Dr. Erickson used inferences when he was working with patients. Here are three examples: I asked one of his former patients about her experience in the first session with him. She was stunned by his observation, which was true. He told her, "You are not your mother's favorite, but I imagine that you are your grandmother's favorite, probably your maternal grandmother."

Years ago, I was invited to a birthday party for a woman who was turning 70. One of her friends, a social worker, approached me because she knew I was the Director of The Milton H. Erickson Foundation. She told me about her first meeting with Dr. Erickson. As soon as she entered the room, he told her that she had most likely spent several of her formative years in a concentration camp. Astonished by the accuracy of his pronouncement, she asked how he knew that. He said it was the way in which she held her body.

A related example was recounted by a therapist who visited Dr. Erickson. He asked her to write down identifying information. As she was writing, he told her that it was highly probable that she did not grow up in the United States. She didn't give much credence to his speculation. Perhaps he saw her handwriting, which would differ from the handwriting of someone reared in the States. He next suggested that she was born in southern Europe. She didn't think much of this observation either. Her ethnicity could be surmised from her features. But then he said, "And you were fat when you were a child." Well, that shocked her, because at the time she was not overweight. When she asked how he came to that conclusion, he replied that it was the way she held her body.

In all three cases, Dr. Erickson's inference was on target. I'm certain that was not always the case. However, if a therapist makes accurate inferences early on, it is likely to empower future interventions. Incorrect inferences will most likely be forgotten.

From time to time I practice making inferences. Perhaps I detect a nuance in someone's voice. I might secretly guess about the person's birth order or where the person was reared. Then, I state my speculation to see if I am correct.

Psychoaerobic Exercise 12 was designed so that students have another opportunity to practice the state of inference.

EXPERIENTIAL EMPOWERMENT
PSYCHOAEROBIC$_{SM}$ Exercises
www.psychoaerobic.org

PSYCHOAEROBIC EXERCISE 12

Clinician Posture to Develop: Extrapolate from minimal cues; predict from minimal cues.

Format: Dyads.

Roles: One person is the Subject; one is the Receiver/Extrapolator.

Method:

Condition One: Participants sit back-to-back. For 3-5 minutes, the Subject verbally describes her office/work space. The Extrapolator enters an acuity state and can ask questions about the work environment. The Extrapolator is not told in advance the content of the inferences that he will make.

Once the description is finished, the Extrapolator makes five guesses about the subject's bedroom. The Extrapolator can infer things, for example:

1. A general description the bedroom, such as if there's modern or antique furniture, or it is crowded or spacious.
2. A description of objects on the bedroom dresser or shelf.
3. Whether or not the closet is organized.
4. The kinds of objects hanging on the bedroom walls—posters, photos, art, religious items, etc.
5. The Extrapolator makes a specific prediction about the bedroom. Is there a TV? Are there candles, books, photographs?

Condition Two: Participants reverse roles and sit face-to-face. The new Subject subvocally describes his office/work space for 3-5 minutes. No sounds are made and the Subject uses normal facial expressions and gestures. All words are mouthed, as if spoken. The Extrapolator answers the following questions regarding the Subject:

1. Where does the Subject fall within his family structure—the oldest; in the middle; the youngest; an only child?
2. Does the Subject exercise regularly?
3. Does the Subject like animals? If so, what kind?
4. Did the Subject grow up in an urban or rural environment?
5. What is the Subject's favorite room at home?
6. What are the Subject's hobbies?
7. What was the major trauma the Subject experienced in her formative years?
8. What is the Subject's most common bad feeling?
9. The Extrapolator creates a prediction about the Subject, e.g., does the person enjoy shopping? Who is the person's favorite family member? On average, how many hours of sleep does the person get every night?

Variations:

1. The Extrapolator describes the cues and processes used to create inferences.
2. Extrapolators indicate how they could be more effective at extrapolating from details in the future; and, in retrospect, what they have might have noticed and inferred.
3. Conduct the extrapolation portion of the exercise by only visually observing the Subject, without the initial description of the person's work space.
4. A member of the group who excels at extrapolating can be identified. Group members can strive to learn his strategies and states.
5. In Condition One or Two, the Subject makes predictions about the Extrapolator without any prior information.

Purpose: To notice patterns and extrapolate from minimal cues. Develop the state of inference.

Discussion: Psychoaerobic Exercise 12

How might one make an inference about childhood trauma? A dear friend of mine, Ayala Pines, (1945-2012) was an Israeli social psychologist, and one of the early investigators of the phenomenon of burnout. She conducted a study (Pines, 2002) in which she surveyed three occupational groups – nurses, teachers, and business people. She asked them why they chose their profession. In summary, nurses chose their profession to be helpful; teachers, to inspire; and business people, to compete and come out on top. These choices were existential goals that affected the way in which stress and burnout were experienced.

Members of each of the three occupational groups could cope adequately with stress, as long as they were meeting their existential goals. Burnout happened when the subjects were thwarted from realizing existential goals, perhaps because of their own lack of skill, or due to stumbling blocks in the work environment. Burnout happened when the nurses could not help, the teachers could not inspire, and the business people could not be the best. It was not stress that caused burnout; it was a failure to meet existential goals.

But then, Dr. Pines conducted an additional survey regarding the participants' backgrounds. She found that in formative years the most common childhood trauma for nurses was being raised in a chaotic environment. For teachers, the most common childhood trauma was embarrassment. Perhaps they were clumsy or overly concerned about some facial feature. In their formative years, business people were most often traumatized by competition. Occupational choices were influenced by upbringing and early trauma. In contrast to their upbringing, the nurses chose an environment that was orderly and controlled. Teachers were most often in front of people and closely observed, and businesspeople competed to be the best. Therefore, one's chosen occupation became a crucible for healing childhood trauma. Hence, by learning one's occupation, extrapolations about childhood trauma can be made using inferential thinking.

Inference is a pattern of "If X, then "Y." For example, if this person is a teacher, perhaps he was traumatized by being significantly embarrassed at an early age. Erickson was a master of inferential thinking. Inference is one of the most important acuity states to develop.

Developing the state of inference can be a matter of practice, failure, and more practice. In literature, an icon of inference is Sherlock Holmes. But, he had to practice to develop his skill. In the opening of the *Hound of the Baskervilles*, Holmes and Watson find a cane. Meticulously studying the cane's markings, they create a profile of the owner. When the owner arrives to claim his cane, Holmes and Watson discover where they erred, and they carefully review their inferential thinking to refine their approach.

Details of a person's most common bad feeling may be inferred. When people are stymied, they commonly express a specific bad feeling. Take for example, being in traffic: Some people will be angry, others fearful, others frustrated, etc. As Eric Berne proposed, transactional sequences often lead to the same emotional ending (the racket). Familiarity is a great motivator in human behavior. People may opt for a familiar bad feeling, even though it is not an adaptive emotional response.

What about family structure and environmental upbringing? Does this factor into a person's behavior? How does it affect the experience of time? Those who grow up in an urban environment may have more of an orientation of immediacy: "I want it now." Those who are reared in the country may have an ingrained sense of seasonal change: "Time may be needed for things to develop."

Dr. Erickson commonly requested information from his patients about their family structure. He also asked whether they grew up in a rural or urban environment. Other than that, he asked for little background information before intervening. Assessment would result from the client's response to preceding interventions. Rather than engaging in a lengthy process of evaluation, the patient would immediately be involved in the process of change. In the case of medical conditions, it is not possible to proceed without diagnostic information, but in a social context, intervention can precede assessment.

Having counseled a number of Dr. Erickson's previous patients, I can relate two examples of his rural orientation. An 18-year-old, newly married woman, who I will call Jane, consulted Dr. Erickson because she was falling down. There was no neurological explanation. Jane had artistic leanings and married a domineering and controlling man employed in a technical field. Jane had problems standing up for herself in her marriage. Dr. Erickson did not make that interpretation, which would have been right, but likely ineffective. He suggested that the couple divorce, implying they were not suited for each other. However, they wanted to remain together for religious reasons, so Dr. Erickson engaged them in family planning. Jane's symptoms ameliorated within a few months and she quickly became pregnant. Dr. Erickson told her she did not need more therapy at that time, but advised that when she entered her 40s, she might seek more therapy.

Why could Dr. Erickson make that prediction? As a farm boy, he understood seasons. As a psychiatrist, he recognized that problems cluster at transition points in the human lifecycle. Jay Haley was one of the first to point out this fact. He made it a focal point in his seminal book, *Uncommon Therapy* (1973), when he grouped Erickson's cases at transition points, such as the birth of child, when the child first goes to school, and when a young adult leaves home.

When Jane entered her 40s, she called Dr. Erickson for consultation. However, Dr. Erickson had passed away, so Mrs. Erickson referred her to me. Again, Jane was falling. Her children had left home and she could no longer stand up for herself in her marriage. Cueing on Dr. Erickson's orientation, I counseled Jane to establish a hobby. I suggested she breed dogs, and subsequently she made a satisfactory life adjustment and stopped falling.

The second example of Dr. Erickson's rural orientation involved me. I had a conversation with Dr. Erickson about the microdynamics of a particular induction that he had conducted during a teaching seminar. (See *A Teaching Seminar with Milton Erickson*, Zeig, 1980.) We suspended the consultation to take a photograph with his infant grandchild, Laurel. Laurel's mother, Roxanna, and Mrs. Erickson would also be in the picture. I was the photographer, but at Dr. Erickson's insistence, I could not take the picture until Mrs. Erickson went back into the house to get the Ironwood sculpture of an owl that Dr. Erickson had gifted to Laurel to celebrate her birth. Then, sitting in his wheelchair, Dr. Erickson cradled Laurel and displayed the owl. He was in the middle with Mrs. Erickson on one side and Roxanna on the other.

When we resumed the consultation, Dr. Erickson explained his strategic thinking. Laurel was nicknamed "Screech" because of her powerful, owl-like cry. Dr. Erickson said that 16 years later, when he was long gone, Laurel would see the photo. There would be a mix of feelings and memories from childhood to her adolescence. He thought that the simple addition of the Ironwood owl added a tremendous amount of humanness to the photograph. The owl was a seed that would have future impact.

Dr. Erickson's strategic thinking reflected his upbringing as a farm boy. A small seed might take years to grow before it would bear fruit. Having a temporal orientation can be a great benefit to clinicians. Some interventions can only be affected in the proper season. Erickson's perspective mirrored the orientation of his father, a farmer, who planted saplings in his 90s because he wanted to see them bear fruit.

Temporal orientations can be useful clues in inferring upbringing. Therapeutic interventions are best when they are tailored. For example, metaphors chosen for therapy with an urban person should be different from those selected for a rural person.

It is possible that birth order can be inferred from a sample of behavior. There is considerable research about how birth order affects personality. Those who are interested can reference the work of Frank Sulloway, who wrote, *Born to Rebel* (1996). Older children may be shyer, and more intellectual and traditional. Middle children may be more on the rebellious end of the spectrum, while younger children may be more compliant. Although these trends often hold, many factors are at play in creating personality. Still, in the workshops that I teach for therapists, there seems to be a preponderance of students who are older children. In their formative years, perhaps they were caretakers of younger siblings (or their parents), which led them into a profession in which caretaking is central.

EXPERIENTIAL EMPOWERMENT
PSYCHOAEROBIC$_{SM}$ Exercises
www.psychoaerobic.org

PSYCHOAEROBIC EXERCISE 13

Clinician Posture to Develop: Extrapolate from minimal cues; develop analogical thinking.

Format: Dyads using the same partners used in Exercise 12. Exercises 12 and 13 can be carried out consecutively.

Roles: Each person is both an Observer/Extrapolator and Subject.

Method: Each person independently describes him- or herself analogically on paper using the following categories.

"As a_____I would be_____________."
1.) Beverage
2.) Article of Clothing
3.) Piece of Furniture
4.) Piece of Art
5.) Part of the Body

After each person has described himself, participants compose a second list answering the question: How do you think your partner would describe you using the following categories?
1.) Beverage
2.) Article of Clothing
3.) Piece of Furniture
4.) Piece of Art
5.) Part of the Body

After each person has described himself, participants compose a third list answering the question: How would you describe your partner using the following categories?

1.) Beverage
2.) Article of Clothing
3.) Piece of Furniture
4.) Piece of Art
5.) Part of the Body

Each partner shares analogical perceptions. What cues helped you to make guesses about your partner? What states did you access?

Variations:

Conduct the exercise with a stranger. Take a few moments to observe the person.

Use in couples therapy to promote engagement.

Purpose: To develop analogical thinking; to notice patterns and extrapolate from those patterns.

EXPERIENTIAL EMPOWERMENT
PSYCHOAEROBIC$_{SM}$ Exercises
www.psychoaerobic.org

PSYCHOAEROBIC EXERCISE 14

Clinician Posture to Develop: Develop alertness to multiple incoming data.

Format: Triads.

Roles: Two Pitchers; one Receiver.

Method: The Receiver sits between the Pitchers. The Pitchers direct their remarks to the Receiver. Each Pitcher chooses a topic and engages the Receiver in a conversation, as if the other Pitcher did not exist. It is best to speak slower than one would normally. The Receiver must converse with both the Pitchers fluently by responding and initiating when necessary, without excluding either Pitcher. In effect, the Receiver holds one conversation on two topics. The Pitchers only converse with the Receiver. Participants should avoid asking questions, which tends to create two separate conversations.

Variation: At the cue of the group leader, the roles are rotated (the Receiver becomes a Pitcher, and one of the Pitchers becomes a Receiver).

Purpose: To develop experientially an ability to process multiple incoming data.

Adapted from Viola Spolin, *Theater Games for Rehearsal,* and Viola Spolin, *Improvisation for the Theater.*

(Handout is given to participants after completing the exercise.)

EXPERIENTIAL EMPOWERMENT
PSYCHOAEROBIC$_{SM}$ Exercises
www.psychoaerobic.org

PSYCHOAEROBIC EXERCISE 15

Clinician Posture to Develop: Acuity to the shaping effect of preconceptions.

Format: Fishbowl.

Roles: One member is selected to be the Pitcher.

Method: The observers access an acuity state. The Pitcher is secretly instructed to tell an ambiguous story about her child, Terry, and is not to indicate whether Terry is a boy or a girl. After the story, the observers write their thoughts/predictions about the subject --Terry's age; appearance, hobbies, temperament, and finally, Terry's sex.

Purpose: In the subsequent discussion, observers may realize the effect of preconceptions on observation.

Discussion: Psychoaerobic Exercise 15

Our preconceptions are brain scripts that help us quickly evaluate how to behave adaptively. Most often, they are effective. Sometimes preconceptions limit choices. This exercise was determined from a case that Dr. Erickson discussed with me that was recorded in *Experiencing Erickson* (Zeig, 1985). A psychopathic patient manipulated her therapist by talking at length about her child who had a name that could be either male or female without disclosing the child's sex. The patient was being manipulative for the sake of manipulation.

Dr. Erickson advised students to come to the session with a beginner's mind, attempting to understand the patient without preconceived techniques and theories that could be limiting. In 1978, when I asked Dr.

Erickson for a quote for the brochure for the first International Congress on Ericksonian Approaches to Hypnosis and Psychotherapy, he wrote: "Each person is an individual. Hence, psychotherapy should be formulated to meet the uniqueness of the individual's needs, rather than tailoring the person to fit the Procrustean bed of a hypothetical theory of human behavior." Our cherished theories may provide valuable focus, but that focus may limit options.

SUMMARY: PSYCHOAEROBIC EXERCISES 3-15

Perceptiveness is highly valued in many professions and life circumstances. Developing acuity is a lifelong pursuit for psychotherapists. Acuity, however, is a concept that must be developed experientially. It cannot be taught with didactic algorithms. It is a way of being in the world; it is not a technique.

Acuity is a meta-category. It is a complexity, a compilation of substates, not a single thing. It is best to pursue components, such as attention to detail, attention to interactions, and concentration. Access enough components and the category will be realized. Experiential exercises can be fashioned for each component. By doing so, an associational network is created that can generate the realization of the concept: "I can be more perceptive." The concept can mature into a state—the state of acuity: "I am being more perceptive." Subsequently, an identity is realized: "I am a perceptive person."

Specific acuity exercises have been composed to develop distinct acuity substates. The exercises address distinct conceptual domains. As a person realizes a sufficient number of concepts, the category and concomitant identity is achieved.

In Psychoaerobic Exercises 3-15, acuity is divided into 12 concepts:

- Perceiving redundancy.
- Understanding and utilizing ambiguity.
- Starting with a beginner's mind. Overcoming the tendency to distort reality according to preconceptions.
- Realizing how minimal changes can profoundly alter meaning.
- Perceiving visual detail.
- Developing auditory concentration.
- Developing visual concentration.
- Perceiving auditory and visual patterns.
- Recognizing interaction patterns. (When "X," then "Y.")
- Attending to conspicuous absences.
- Developing inferential skills (If "X," then "Y.") Extrapolating from

minimal cues.
- Attending to and performing with multiple incoming data.

These Psychoaerobic Exercises were developed to access components of acuity. It is a rare person who can effectively access every component at his or her disposal. By engaging in all the exercises, individuals can realize strengths, and focus on improving weaknesses.

Although acuity is only one state that therapists can develop, the greatest number of exercises in this book falls into this category. As a whole, the acuity exercises serve as a holographic model for the entire Psychoaerobic system, which consists of experientially accessing components to elicit a meta-category. It is also a model of how to intervene in therapy. Consider how the model underlying the acuity exercises can be generalized for problems and solutions. As examples, let's return to depression and happiness.

From one vantage point, depression can be considered a disease. But, from the perspective of social construction, the diagnosis of "depression" is a meta-category, a construct of convenience that allows for ease of communicating a complexity. Depression can be considered a syndrome, not a singularity: It is composed of a number of components unique to an individual. For example, a person could consider himself depressed when he is suffers from a compilation of the following components: being internally preoccupied, feeling low energy, being absorbed in dark thoughts and memories, feeling unable to take pleasure in simple moments, being socially withdrawn, lacking compelling goals, believing that he is a victim of circumstances, and being negative. Another individual could embody only three or four of these components and still report being depressed. In any case, in composing a social intervention, it's more efficacious to treat components, than to address the category.

Similarly, happiness is a construct of convenience. It could consist of the following components: being visually aware, feeling energetic, having pleasant thoughts and memories, taking pleasure in simple moments, being socially engaged, pursuing meaningful goals, believing that one is a hero in one's social drama, and being positive. An individual would not have to manifest all of these components to believe that he is happy. It is a matter of realizing a sufficient number of components. When a threshold is achieved, it can activate realization of the concept and concomitant state and identity.

Therapists can experientially elicit components to prompt activation of the overall category. A focus on generating specific conceptual realizations can bring forth global change. In simpler terms, therapists can help patients become happier people by activating substates. Once the depressed patient realizes that he is laughing more, socially engaging more, being attentive to the external world, and so forth, he will begin to embody the persona of a happy person. Clinicians can map the patient's problem into components and devise experiential tasks that elicit desired components. This procedure allows the patient to energize and change the category from something negative to something positive.

The Psychoaerobic Exercises are designed to model states that were intrinsic to Dr. Erickson. So far, we have explored three states: being experiential, orienting toward, and acuity. The exercises that follow develop additional Ericksonian concepts and states and address a new category – Being Strategic.

PSYCHOAEROBIC EXERCISES 16-24:
An Introduction

In 1973, Jay Haley introduced the concept of strategic therapy, noting that therapy is strategic when a therapist has a goal in mind and works toward that outcome. His proclamation was in contradistinction to the prevailing zeitgeist, which centered on psychoanalytic and humanistic approaches based respectively on insight and immediate experience. Haley's strategic therapy was heavily influenced by Erickson, who was his mentor, and who used strategic development in ways that had not been previously applied in psychotherapy. Erickson's plan was to strengthen realization of the conceptual goal by intentionally proceeding in a stepwise manner.

Strategic development is essential to conceptual communication. The nature of much artistic communication is strategic. Scriptwriters employ the technique of "setup and payoff." Composers use strategic development to elaborate musical themes. Orators use it to build to a denouement. For therapists, it is not a matter of whether or not to be strategic. Therapists must be strategic when the intent involves eliciting states. Composing a well-formed outcome is the first step.

Decades ago, in one of my acting classes, I had a memorable lesson in outcome-oriented thinking. Students were given written monologues to memorize, rehearse, and present. (Of course, the monologue is the actor's calling card at auditions.) When it was my turn, I woodenly stood before the class and began to recite my lines. The instructor stopped me midsentence: "Jeff, what is your intent?" I explained that I was a good student and that my goal was to correctly recite my lines. But she prodded me to think about the effect that I wanted to have on the audience. What emotions did I want to elicit? Did I want the audience to laugh? Be on my side? Feel my angst? This led to an epiphany. Before launching into a hypnotic induction, I would first clarify in my mind the strategic effect I wanted to achieve. And before offering an intervention in non-hypnotic therapy, I would orient similarly.

But the teacher had not completed her constructive criticism. Pressing further she explained, "Jeff, you're not using your body." "My body? I'm supposed to use my body?" My psychotherapy teachers and supervisors implied that clinicians did not use their bodies to augment therapeutic directives. The implication was that the power of therapy comes from unadulterated words. Up until that point, I mirrored my mentors, sitting rigidly in my therapist chair, restricting gestures to adhere to the traditional training standard. But after the improvisation class, I began strategically using gestures and expressions during the therapy sessions I offered. I also used nonverbal communication in hypnotic inductions, even while a client had his eyes closed. The intent is to strengthen directives. Some nuanced micro examples with Dr. Erickson are illustrative:

I remember sheepishly calling Dr. Erickson in the mid-1970s to arrange a visit to see him in Phoenix. I was shy and obsessed for some time before summoning the courage to call. When I finally called, Dr. Erickson answered. Hesitantly, I said, "Dr. Erickson, this is Jeff Zeig." "Jeff!" he exclaimed, as if greeting a dear friend.

If you watch one of the videos of Dr. Erickson conducting a hypnotic induction, you will see that oftentimes he is smiling, even though his client has his eyes closed. His smile was strategically designed to communicate his pleasure in seeing his patient's accomplishment.

Dr. Erickson was the most intentional therapeutic communicator I have ever encountered. He composed his communication in a way that is comparable to the method of a poet—every word, every gesture, was crafted for strategic effect.

It's hard to believe that sculpted, micro-interventions could be intentionally composed during the ebb and flow of a clinical hour, but Dr. Erickson did just that. In 1980, I edited, *A Teaching Seminar with Milton H. Erickson*. The book was basically a transcript of one of Dr. Erickson's week-long training courses. Dr. Erickson spoke grammatically correct sentences, which meant that the book needed very little editing.

The appendix to that book consists of a transcript of a five-hour discussion between Dr. Erickson and me about the intricacies of a 50-minute hypnotic induction he had conducted during the seminar. In our discussion (which took place several months after the seminar) he analyzed every nuance and indicated his intent.

At one point in the analysis I turned off the videotape for an inquiry. Dr. Erickson interjected: "She's going to talk about her paralyzed arm." The subject, let's call her, Sally, had her left arm hypnotically paralyzed earlier in the induction. There were two purposes: her paralyzed arm was a hypnotic phenomenon that served as a convincer of trance. It was also placed symbolically to suggest self-protection, an underlying therapeutic theme. It did not seem possible that Dr. Erickson would remember such an obscure detail about Sally's conversation after so many months. I asked him to explain his inference. He told me to replay the tape. He then pointed out a moment in which he intentionally moved his left arm an inch or two. It was just before I turned off the tape. He surmised that Sally would see his movement in her peripheral vision, which would prompt her to think about, and then talk about, her paralyzed arm. That turned out to be the case. (The video of this session, with my accompanying commentary entitled *Resistance*, can be ordered from the Erickson Foundation store at www.ericksonfoundationstore.com.)

As a remarkably precise communicator, Dr. Erickson worked tirelessly to fashion the total weave of his communication to garner his intended response. The effect of his efforts on those with whom he consulted was profound. The result for me was that I never felt so loved in my life. It was Dr. Erickson's extraordinary precision and intentionality that created that effect. No person in my previous experience had worked so assiduously to reach me.

Psychoareobic Exercises 16-24 are designed to elicit the concept/state of intentionally communicating for strategic effect. Both verbal and paraverbal methods are explored. Some of the exercises are composed by using the technique of isolating specific modalities. Again, consider the analogy of a gym where exercise equipment isolates certain muscle groups to promote their development.

Other aspects of strategic communication include strengthening the message by making the presentation dense and multilevel, and layering elements to additionally empower the goal. For example, if a therapist is being traditionally empathic, his verbal reflection can be strengthened by using changes in vocal characteristics, adding complementary gestures, using an analogy, etc. Think of music composition where the simple technique of doubling a note or adding grace notes adds to the effect. In composing his Fifth Symphony, Beethoven takes a simple theme and makes it come alive by modifying rhythm, timbre, and harmony, and by adding and deleting instruments. Increasing the density of the communication is a royal road for eliciting concepts, states, and identities.

One of Dr. Erickson's most important contributions was his in-depth exploration of strengthening methods. Strengthening the message is a desirable therapist state that can be accessed whenever the intended message is phenomenological and consists of an emotion, concept, or state.

There are myriad ways in which to strengthen a conceptual message. The following exercises present ways in which the message can be strengthened microdynamically, using gestures, touch, sounds, sequential development, orienting toward, providing a motivation, creating attributions, harnessing prosody, and making changes in voice, tone, and tempo. There are also macrodynamic ways of strengthening a message, by applying hypnosis through storytelling, by tailoring, etc. (See Zeig, 2014 for examples.)

Some exercises in the next set can be used in supervision or in clinical role-playing. But, the primary intent for these exercises is to help clinicians develop the concepts/states of being strategic and strengthening the message. After the exercises, participants should discuss how to identify and improve these therapist states.

EXPERIENTIAL EMPOWERMENT
PSYCHOAEROBIC$_{SM}$ Exercises
www.psychoaerobic.org

PSYCHOAEROBIC EXERCISE 16

Clinician Posture to Develop: Communicate for strategic effect; orient toward; develop implicit responsiveness.

Format: Triads.

Roles: Two Pitchers. One Receiver. The Receiver is told that mild touch will be used and provides permission in advance.

Method: The Receiver closes his eyes. The Receiver is not told the goal of the Pitchers. The Pitchers enter the state of orienting toward, and consecutively communicate relaxation. Pitcher One communicates relaxation solely with verbal methods, restricting the use of gesture and paraverbal markers. Each verbal intervention must be an allusion to relaxation. The word "relaxation" or its synonyms cannot be used. For example, the pitcher can talk about the climate in the room: "You might notice stillness in the air." "The warmth in the room can be pleasing." "There can be a curious sense of fully attending to a sense of heaviness in the air," etc. Pitcher Two communicates relaxation solely with touch. For example, placing her hands lightly on the Receiver's shoulders, and then gently pressing down. Each intervention is brief: one or two sentences if verbal; one distinct intervention if nonverbal. The exercise is continued for 10-15 interventions each before it concludes. Discuss the state of orienting toward.

Variations:
1. At the signal of the group leader, the Pitchers reverse roles.
2. At the signal of the group leader, the Pitchers communicate simultaneously.

3. The goal can be altered: There can be a "hypnotic" goal, such as modified attention, altered intensity, or the experience of dissociation. (See Zeig, 2014 for more information.)
4. The goal could be any emotion, concept, or state—happiness, motivation, or curiosity, etc.
5. Change roles so that each member of the triad has a turn.

Purpose: The Pitchers isolate and develop verbal and nonverbal methods to gift-wrap the goal. The Receiver develops responsiveness to verbal and nonverbal methods. The suggestions are strengthened through allusions and nonverbal methods.

EXPERIENTIAL EMPOWERMENT
PSYCHOAEROBIC$_{SM}$ Exercises
www.psychoaerobic.org

PSYCHOAEROBIC EXERCISE 17

Clinician Posture to Develop: Communicate for strategic effect. Multilevel communication.

Format: Triads.

Roles: One Pitcher; one Receiver; one Coach.

Method: The Receiver closes his eyes. The Pitcher offers a hypnotic induction to elicit relaxation, pausing between sentences. (If the participants are not conversant with hypnosis, progressive relaxation can be substituted.) When the Pitcher pauses, the Coach asks the Pitcher to augment the communication by adding a specific extra-verbal component, e.g., "Next, communicate relaxation by adding a gesture." "...by adding a facial expression." "...by adding movement." "...by adding a posture." "...by adding prosody to your voice." "...by changing your breathing rate." "...by adding a sound." "...by adding a change in proximity." The process continues for 10-15 discrete interventions.

Discuss the state of using multilevel communication

Variations:

1. The group leader directs the Pitcher and Coach to change roles and continue the process.
2. In place of relaxation, the goal could be an emotion, concept, or one of the phenomenological aspects of hypnosis, e.g., alter attention, modify intensity, promote dissociation, or elicit implicit responsiveness. (For more information, see Zeig, 2014).)_
3. Use one of the instructions in the reorientation process, e.g., "Communicate reorientation and add a gesture."

Purpose: To learn experientially what it is like to strategically augment communication with nonverbal methods.

Adapted from Viola Spolin, *Improvisation for the Theater*.

EXPERIENTIAL EMPOWERMENT
PSYCHOAEROBIC$_{SM}$ Exercises
www.psychoaerobic.org

PSYCHOAEROBIC EXERCISE 18A

Clinician Posture to Develop: Communicate for strategic effect. Multilevel communication.

Format: Dyads.

Roles: One Pitcher; one Receiver.

Method: The Receiver is told to expect two brief but similar hypnotic inductions and is asked to leave the room so that the Pitcher can receive further instructions in private. (Alternatively, this handout can be given to the Pitcher to read before proceeding.) The Pitcher is to offer two similar inductions and awaken the Receiver briefly between the inductions. Each induction can consist of 10 simple absorption (e.g., progressive relaxation) suggestions and five ratification instructions. (See Zeig, 2014 for more information.) The only difference between the two inductions is that the Pitcher deliberately and intermittently smiles during one induction, and does not smile during the other. The smile should indicate, "I am happy to see your pleasure/accomplishment.". (An induction script that can be used is provided below.)

After both inductions are completed, the Receiver reports the experiential difference between them. The Receiver is asked, "Which induction did you like best, and why?" Subsequently, the Receiver is debriefed.

Induction Script
You can close your eyes...
You can take a deep breath...
You can focus inside...so you can...explore inside...
And you can...discover patterns of comfort...

And I don't know where the comfort is now most interesting and increasingly vivid...

Perhaps you can...appreciate the comfort... in your legs...

Perhaps you can...explore the comfort... in your body...

Perhaps you can...enjoy the comfort... in your head...

And you can't realize all the ways...the comfort can evolve...

But your unconscious mind can help you...realize the changing patterns...

And while I've been talking to you,

Your breathing rate has changed...

Your pulse rate has altered...

Your swallowing reflex is different...

Your motor movements have changed...

Your blink rate has altered...

Now, take one or two or three deep breaths...and completely reorient yourself...all over.

Discuss the states for both the Pitcher and Receiver.

Variations:

1. In one induction, the Pitcher does not smile. Instead, she randomly makes an approval sound: "Aah."
2. While the Receiver's eyes are closed, the Pitcher conducts one of the inductions by using one incongruent method, e.g., holding his right toe, holding his thumb on his nose, or occasionally yawning.
3. The Pitcher does not expect the Receiver to achieve the goal in one iteration, but does expect the Receiver to achieve the goal in the other iteration.
4. In one induction, after the Receiver closes his eyes, the Pitcher makes gestures complementary to the verbal suggestions.
5. In one induction the Pitcher makes various gestures that are opposite of the verbal suggestions.

Purpose: To realize the subtle effect of gesture. To build responsiveness to gesture. To realize the shaping effect of implicit attributions.

EXPERIENTIAL EMPOWERMENT
PSYCHOAEROBIC$_{SM}$ Exercises
www.psychoaerobic.org

PSYCHOAEROBIC EXERCISE 18B

Clinical Posture to Develop: Communicate for strategic effect. Attributions.

Format: Dyads.

Roles: One Pitcher; one Receiver. Reverse roles from Psychoaerobic Exercise 18A.

Method: The Receiver is told to expect two brief but similar inductions, and then is asked to leave the room so that the Pitcher can privately receive further instructions. (Alternatively, the handout can be given solely to the Pitcher.) The Pitcher offers two iterations (similar to Exercise 18A). During the first induction, after the Receiver closes his eyes, the Pitcher paces the breathing rate of the Receiver and moves closer to the Receiver. In the second induction (also with eyes closed), the Pitcher does not pace his breathing and remains at a distance.

In the discussion period immediately after awakening, the Pitcher creates strong attributions by emphatically and sincerely stating that there were overt signs of increased depth in the induction where the Pitcher remains at a distance. Then, and only then, the Receiver is asked to note the experiential difference between the inductions. At the end of the discussion, the Pitcher debriefs and divulges to the Receiver the changes made in breathing rate and proximity. Both discuss the effect of the attributions.

Induction Script

Close your eyes...

You can go inside...

You can notice a concentration of comfort...in your body...

Perhaps you can...notice your feet...balanced...on the ground...

And as you take a deep breath, you can...concentrate on the developing warmth and comfort in your feet...and legs...that is so easy...to realize...

And as you realize warmth and comfort...in your legs, you can take another easy breath...and allow the comfort and warmth to...develop even more.... in your body...

And you can't realize all the ways...the warmth and comfort can be realized in your arms...and hands...

And as you notice those feelings—comfort and warmth...

And as you realize those feelings—warmth and comfort...

You can take an easy breath and allow the comfort and warmth to... concentrate...in your mind...

And while I've been talking to you certain changes occur...

There may be a wholehearted warmth...in the center of your body...

Your head may be in a different place than it was before...

Your feet may seem farther from your head...

Your shoulders may feel lighter...

There may be a coolness developing around your temples...

Now take one or two or three deep breaths...and completely reorient yourself...all over.

Variation: The Pitcher offers two identical inductions. The Pitcher can indicate that there were greater signs of depth in one of the inductions, preferably the one in which the Receiver seemed least absorbed. In the discussion immediately following awakening, he empathically and sincerely insists that there were differences between the inductions, for example, by stating, "You went deeper in the (first/second) induction. There were four indicators: 1.) your breathing rate was slower; 2.) your pulse rate altered; 3.) your swallowing reflex changed; and 4.) your eyes showed more rapid eye movement (REM)." This could be followed by: "Why did you go deeper?" "What specifically did I do differently in that induction to promote increased depth?"

Then, and only then, the Pitcher allows the Receiver to discuss the experiential difference between the inductions. After the discussion, the Receiver is debriefed. Perhaps the Receiver will inadvertently present attributions to the Pitcher, insisting, "No, you were very different in the first induction." The purpose of this variation is to study the effect of attributions.

Purpose: Realize the subtle effect of paraverbal communication. Build responsiveness. Attune. Discover the shaping effect of attributions.

EXPERIENTIAL EMPOWERMENT
PSYCHOAEROBIC$_{SM}$ Exercises
www.psychoaerobic.org

PSYCHOAEROBIC EXERCISE 19

Clinician Posture to Develop: To develop analogical thinking; present a multilevel message; to realize the effect of preconceptions.

Format: Dyads.

Roles: One Pitcher; one Receiver.

Method: The Pitcher and Receiver are each given instructions privately. The Receiver is secretly instructed to bring to mind a circumscribed problem, e.g., mild depression, mild anxiety, a parent-child issue. The Receiver is told to expect a powerful, effective induction that will modify the presenting problem. The Receiver does not talk about the problem; he just keeps it in mind as the Pitcher intervenes.

The Pitcher is secretly told to expect a patient whose behavior has been programmed to be subtly passive-aggressive. The Pitcher is given instructions to conduct an imagery induction.

When the participants meet, the Pitcher is to conduct a five-minute imagery induction without any discussion of the problem. The induction centers on imaging a bright red, irregular spike shape, hidden by a fog. The Pitcher is told that the image symbolizes passive-aggressive anger. The induction image is to be used for two purposes: 1.) to fixate attention; and 2.) to symbolically parallel the problem that the Pitcher expects. After creating an induction that absorbs the Receiver in the possible details of the image, the Pitcher slowly and progressively modifies the image by changing its size, adding the color, white, so that the image fades, removing the fog, etc. After the absorption phase, the Pitcher ratifies and then terminates the trance.

In the discussion, the Pitcher is instructed by the group leader to explain to the Receiver how the Receiver behaved passive-aggressively in the initial discussion of hobbies. Then, the Pitcher and Receiver discuss the effect of the intervention in modifying the Receiver's problem. Finally, the role of expectations is discussed and the participants debrief.

Purpose: Learn how preconceptions affect (or do not affect) outcomes.

EXPERIENTIAL EMPOWERMENT
PSYCHOAEROBIC$_{SM}$ Exercises
www.psychoaerobic.org

PSYCHOAEROBIC EXERCISE 20

Clinician Posture to Develop: Communicate for strategic effect. Multilevel communication.

Format: Dyads or Triads.

Roles: One Pitcher (who also serves as Commentator); one Receiver; one Commentator (if triads).

Method: The Receiver closes his eyes. The Receiver is instructed to protect himself from being vulnerable. The Receiver's experience in achieving trance is incidental.

The Pitcher offers an induction of hypnosis, the goal of which can be to elicit relaxation. The Pitcher provides 10-15 simple suggestions, pausing after each. Subsequent to each suggestion, the Pitcher narrates the extra-verbal communication in the first person, past tense, e.g., (1.) "Relax your feet." "As I spoke, I softened the tone of my voice." (2) "Relax your ankles." "As I spoke, I moved my head toward you." The Pitcher can use two different voice tones—one for hypnosis, and another for the commentary.

After the exercise, the Pitcher should summarize to the Receiver what he learned about para-verbal communication. Then, the Receiver can discuss his experience. Remember, the focus of the exercise is to improve the Pitcher's use of multilevel communication.

Variations:

1. Conduct the exercise in triads with a Commentator who narrates the extra-verbal communication of the Pitcher. The Commentator can use "you" statements, e.g., "As you spoke about depth, you lowered your voice tone."

2. The Receiver role-plays a problem. The Pitcher therapeutically intervenes, and narrates extra-verbal elements after each sentence or intervention. Alternatively, conduct the exercise in triads with a Commentator who narrates the para-verbal actions of the Pitcher.
3. The exercise is conducted in triads with two Pitchers and one Receiver. After Pitcher One intervenes, Pitcher Two narrates Pitcher One's extra-verbal elements to the Receiver, e.g., "Now he is moving his head toward you." Then, Pitcher Two offers an intervention and Pitcher One narrates. The process continues until each Pitcher offers 10-15 suggestions, at which time the trance is terminated.
4. The exercise is conducted in triads with a Commentator who narrates the actions of the Pitcher and the Receiver.
5. In the narration, the Commentator emphasizes interactional response patterns, e.g., "As you (Pitcher) moved forward, she (Receiver) took a deep breath and relaxed her shoulders," or "When you (Pitcher) slowed your speech, she (Receiver) slowed her breathing," or "When you (Receiver) moved forward, she (Pitcher) also moved forward.
6. For the first five interventions, the Commentator narrates extra-verbal elements; for the next five interventions, the Commentator narrates patterns of responsive behavior, e.g., "When he said/did 'X,' you did 'Y.'"
7. The exercise is conducted in a group of four—with a Pitcher and a Receiver, both of whom have a personal Commentator.

Purpose: The Pitcher explores extra-verbal elements and their strengthening effect.

Adapted from Viola Spolin, *Improvisation for the Theater*.

EXPERIENTIAL EMPOWERMENT
PSYCHOAEROBIC$_{SM}$ Exercises
www.psychoaerobic.org

PSYCHOAEROBIC EXERCISE 21

Clinician Posture to Develop: Communicate for effect. Multilevel communication.

Format: Triads.

Roles: Two Pitchers; one Receiver.

Method: The Receiver closes his eyes. The Pitchers speak slowly and consecutively using gibberish to induce hypnosis in the Receiver. Pitcher One uses gibberish to communicate aspects of relaxation. Pitcher Two uses gibberish to communicate aspects of slowing down. For example, the suggestion can be to slow down movements, breathing rate, thought process, etc.

It is advisable for the Pitchers to think specifically, e.g., "Slow down what?" "Relax how?" The Pitchers should let their bodies communicate the message—lead with their bodies. Use extra-verbal methods with specific intent.

After the exercise, the participants should discuss what they learned about the effect of modifying para-verbal methods.

Variations:

1. At the signal of the group leader, Pitchers One and Two reverse roles.
2. Combine this exercise with Exercise 20, using a Pitcher who speaks gibberish to induce trance and pauses in between suggestions; a Receiver who goes into trance; and a Commentator who after each suggestion narrates the Pitcher's extra-verbal communication.

3. Make the induction interactional. The Pitchers ask specific gibberish questions. The hypnotized Receiver responds verbally to the best of his ability, trying to discern the meaning of the question.
4. Offer eye closure and reorientation suggestions in gibberish.
5. Pick goals, other than "relaxation" and "slow down," e.g., envision specific imagery or recall vivid childhood memories. Elicit motivation or commitment, etc.
6. Conduct an entire induction using only gibberish.
7. Use tones rather than gibberish.
8. Use a single syllable, e.g. "bah," rather than gibberish.
9. Hum rather than use gibberish.
10. In a role-play, offer a therapeutic intervention using gibberish, tones, or a single syllable, e.g., suggest to the patient to "stop smoking" or "eat less."
11. In a role-play, conduct systematic desensitization or EMDR using gibberish.
12. Work in dyads. The Pitcher chooses one of three possible goals—relaxation, vibrant imagery, or vivid memories—and works in gibberish to specifically achieve one of the goals. The Receiver is not told the goal. After the exercise, ask the Receiver which goal he experienced.
13. Role-play a therapy session where the therapist only responds using sounds like, Aah, Huh, Eee, Ooh, and Ugh." Avoid common ones like, "Uh-huh and Hmm."

Purpose: The Pitchers must isolate and develop nonverbal methods to orient toward the goal. Build responsiveness by using voice tone, tempo, and emphasis (para-verbal methods). Notice the effect of para-verbal communication.

EXPERIENTIAL EMPOWERMENT
PSYCHOAEROBIC$_{SM}$ Exercises
www.psychoaerobic.org

PSYCHOAEROBIC EXERCISE 22

Clinician Posture to Develop: Communicate for strategic effect. Multilevel communication.

Format: Triads or groups of four.

Roles: Two (or three Pitchers); one Receiver.

Method: The Receiver is told that touch may be used in the exercise and provides permission. The Receiver closes her eyes. Each Pitcher induces trance using one word augmented by para-verbal communication. Pitcher One uses "comfort." Pitcher Two uses "focus." (Pitcher Three uses "attend.") The words can be used once, or repeated. The Pitchers can vary para-verbal markers—e.g., tone, tempo, direction of voice, emphasis, and/or touch—to indicate the location, intensity, and duration of the intended effect. During the induction, the Pitchers can move about the room. The Pitchers intervene consecutively. Each Pitcher makes 10 distinct interventions.

Variations:

1. The Pitchers conduct the induction to affect their respective goals, each using a discrete verbal tone or sound, e.g., humming, or tapping.
2. The Pitchers conduct the induction using only touch to communicate alterations in focus, intensity, dissociation, and implicit responsiveness.
3. After a series of consecutive interventions, the Pitchers are instructed by the group leader to intervene simultaneously.
4. The Receiver begins with her eyes opened. Pitcher One's initial

intervention using the concept of "focus" must suggest eye closure.

5. The Receiver goes into trance with her eyes open, thereby allowing the Pitchers to use gesture as cues.
6. Using only one word, the Pitchers must set up and gradually develop a goal response from the Receiver, such as arm levitation.
7. Create reorientation from trance using only the key words "comfort," "focus," and "attend."
8. In a group of five (one patient and four therapists), role-play a complete "therapy," sequentially using the words "focus," "comfort," "remember," and "integrate." Each therapist uses only one word. The patient discusses the problem to be addressed in the role-play. This variation can be done with one therapist who can use any of the four words according to what feels most appropriate at the time.
9. Conduct the exercise in dyads. The Pitcher can only use the word "yes" and the sentence, "That's right." The word or sentence can be repeated as many times as is necessary.
10. Role-play a therapy problem. The therapist can only use the words: "Who, what, when, where, how, why, and why not."

Purpose: The Pitchers must access creativity. The Pitchers must first decide the goal response and then gift-wrap it by using para-verbal methods rather than words.

EXPERIENTIAL EMPOWERMENT
PSYCHOAEROBIC$_{SM}$ Exercises
www.psychoaerobic.org

PSYCHOAEROBIC EXERCISE 23

Clinician Posture to Develop: Communicate for strategic effect. Multilevel communication.

Format: Dyads.

Roles: One Pitcher; one Receiver.

Method: The Pitcher conducts an induction of hypnosis, saying only the following sentence, "You can be yourself absorbed in the experience." The Receiver repeats the sentence, but modifies it to become an "I" statement. For example:

Pitcher: You can be yourself absorbed in the experience.
Receiver: I can be myself absorbed in the experience.

The Pitcher is required to say the sentence 10 times, each time using different emphasis, intonations, pauses, etc. With each repetition the Pitcher should strive to elicit a distinct response. Before saying the sentence, decide the intent, e.g., to elicit memories, sensations, images, etc. Do not use touch in this exercise. Instead, use changes in tone, tempo, and locus of voice to devise a way to say the sentence with a different intent with each rendition.

The Pitcher is allowed to make four changes in the sentence: 1.) add simple qualifiers, such as "really," "completely," and "now"; 2.) occasionally insert the Receiver's name in the sentence; 3.) repeat words within the sentence; and 4.) only use part of the sentence. *Remember that the intent should be decided beforehand.*

Variations:

1. The Receiver does not repeat the Pitcher's sentence and passively accepts the suggestions.
2. Conduct the exercise in triads as a sequential double induction. The second Pitcher says the sentence, "You can, (insert Receiver's name), easily respond to any suggestion of comfort."
3. Conduct the exercise in triads with a Commentator who narrates the Pitcher's extra-verbal communication.
4. Conduct the exercise in triads with a Commentator who narrates the extra-verbal actions of both the Pitcher and Receiver.
5. Conduct the exercise in triads with an "Echo" who sits behind the Receiver. In order to provide feedback, the Echo mirrors back to the Pitcher his words, emphasis, and gestures.
6. Use linkage. Link the suggestions by starting the sentence with the words such as, "and," "or," "but," "while," etc. (See Zeig, 2014, for information about the importance of linkage.)
7. Before saying the sentence, the Pitcher declares his intention in one or two words, e.g., to "relax," "increase depth," "focus inside," "build responsiveness," etc.

Purpose: The Pitcher learns to create and embellish suggestions using para-verbal markers.

EXPERIENTIAL EMPOWERMENT
PSYCHOAEROBIC$_{SM}$ Exercises
www.psychoaerobic.org

PSYCHOAEROBIC EXERCISE 24

Clinician Posture to Develop: Communicate for strategic effect. Multilevel communication.

Format: Triads.

Roles: Person A is the Pitcher and the most experienced of the triad in inducing trance. Person B is the Receiver. Person C is the Shadow and the least experienced in inducing trance.

Method: The Receiver closes her eyes. The Pitcher offers an induction of hypnosis composed of 10-15 sentences (or offers progressive relaxation), pausing after each suggestion to allow time for the Shadow (Echo) to respond. The Shadow immediately feeds back as precisely as possible the content, gesture, and tone, etc. of the Pitcher's suggestion.

Variations:

1. At the direction of the group leader, the Shadow, Pitcher, and Receiver change roles.
2. The Shadow acts as "supervisor" and provides an augmentation of tone, gesture, wording, etc. that could strengthen the Pitcher's message. The Shadow imparts the basic message of the Pitcher and makes minimal, constructive modifications. For example, the Shadow could repeat exactly what the Pitcher said and make one modification in gesture. Alternatively, the Shadow could repeat exactly the Pitcher's gesture and make a small change in the Pitcher's wording. After the Shadow reflects back the Pitcher, the Pitcher can repeat the Shadow's modification(s) and then offer a

new suggestion. The Shadow should only augment the new suggestion, not the repetition.

3. The Shadow augments suggestions to advance hypnotic goals, e.g., alter attention, modify intensity, dissociate, or build responsiveness.

Purpose: The Pitcher and Shadow learn to strengthen the message.

EXPERIENTIAL EMPOWERMENT
PSYCHOAEROBIC$_{SM}$ Exercises
www.psychoaerobic.org

PSYCHOAEROBIC EXERCISE 25

Clinician Posture to Develop: Communicate for strategic effect. Multilevel communication.

Format: Triads.

Roles: One Pitcher; one Receiver; one Dubber. Rotate roles so that each has a turn.

Method: The Receiver closes his eyes. The Pitcher provides an induction of hypnosis. The method is simple pacing and leading, e.g., "You are sitting on the chair and you can close your eyes." "Your feet are resting on the floor and you can slow down your breathing," etc. All suggestions should follow this format. The Pitcher must use gestures with each suggestion, and can mildly exaggerate the use of gesture. The Dubber stands behind the Pitcher. After a short while, the Pitcher stops communicating verbally and only communicates nonverbally. The Pitcher can do this by speaking subvocally, not making any sound. The Dubber provides the words for the Pitcher's actions. The Pitcher must lead with gestures, so that the Dubber can strive to provide the appropriate words. The dubbing is effective when the Pitcher and Dubber act as one. They experience pacing and leading from both verbal and nonverbal perspectives.

Variation: When cued by the group leader, the Pitcher and Dubber change roles.

Purpose: Focus output for desired effect. Enhance the use of gesture.

Adapted from Viola Spolin, *Improvisation for the Theater.*

EXPERIENTIAL EMPOWERMENT
PSYCHOAEROBIC$_{SM}$ Exercises
www.psychoaerobic.org

PSYCHOAEROBIC EXERCISE 26

Clinician Posture to Develop: Being strategic. Strengthen the message.

Format: Triads.

Roles: Two Pitchers; one Receiver.

Method: This is an exercise for practicing the SIFT process (Set up, Intervene, and Follow Through).

The Pitchers elicit goals by harnessing the three-step, strategic process of Pace (Set up), Intervene (Goal), and Motivate (Follow Through). The goal intervention is "sandwiched" between the pacing and motivating steps. Pacing can be accomplished by making a simple, direct truism about a facet of the Receiver's behavior.

There are three goal interventions:

1. Establishing trance. The Pitchers conduct an induction of hypnosis by: (a) eliciting internal absorption; (b) modifying intensity; (c) promoting disassociation; and (d) eliciting responses to minimal cues;
2. Intensifying trance (offering suggestion of increasing involvement/depth)
3. Eliciting vivid memories.

Note that passive verbs are generally used for the intervention.

There can be recursive variations and repetitions of the three goals, but they should be addressed sequentially. Motivation can be accomplished by providing a personalized reason for following the goal. The motivation instruction can be introduced by using the word "because," and then adding a relevant motivation. Prior to the exercise, the Receiver can discuss his personal appreciation of trance, so that the Pitcher can ascertain motivations that can be personalized.

Here are examples of the three-step process:

(Pace) You are looking at me...
(Goal) ...you can close your eyes...
(Motivate) ...because it can be so nice to focus inside.

(Pace) Your eyes are closed...
(Goal)...and you can begin to notice how the comfort inside begins to grow...
(Motivate)...because there are many interesting sensations to explore.

(Pace)...and you may notice the fluttering of your eyelids...
(Goal)...and you can...open your eyes... to many new experiences
(Motivate)... because it is nice to entertain new perspectives.

The exercise is a double induction. After Pitcher One presents the entire "sandwich," Pitcher Two similarly follows.

At the direction of the group leader, change roles so that each participant has a turn. The discussion should focus on describing the state of being strategic.

Variations:

1. The Pitchers strive to establish a relationship that connects the Setup, Intervention, and/or Follow- Through, e.g., "Your hands can relax (Setup), and you can...relax handily (Intervention) because your unconscious mind can hand you (Follow-Through) many delightful opportunities."
2. The Pitchers vary interventions, alternating behavioral and psychological goals. Begin by first using a behavioral goal, e.g., eye closure; next a psychological goal, e.g., establishing comfort; next a behavioral goal, e.g., slowing down the rate of breathing; and next, a psychological goal, e.g., intensifying of comfort.

Purpose: To realize that even simple interventions are strengthened when strategically presented within a dramatic process.

EXPERIENTIAL EMPOWERMENT
PSYCHOAEROBIC$_{SM}$ Exercises
www.psychoaerobic.org

PSYCHOAEROBIC EXERCISE 38

Clinician Posture to Develop: Utilization.

Format: Dyads

Roles: One Pitcher; one Receiver.

Method: The Pitcher conducts an induction using whichever methods she prefers. After establishing the trance, at frequent intervals, the Pitcher asks the Receiver to respond verbally to the ambiguous question, "What are you experiencing right now?" The Pitcher must utilize the response the Receiver provides to compose the subsequent intervention. The Pitcher can target the utilized concept to a trance (or therapy) goal. One way to do this is to take a descriptive concept used by the Receiver and modify it into a trance concept.

The Pitcher can modify the stimulus question through changes in tone or emphasis to take advantage of the fact that a small change in tempo or inflection can significantly alter meaning, e.g., "*What* are you experiencing right now?" "What *are* you experiencing right now?" "What are *you* experiencing right now?" "What are you *experiencing* right now?" "What are you experiencing *right* now?" "What are you experiencing right *now*?"

Example One:

Pitcher: What are you experiencing right now?
Receiver: I hear the fan.]
Pitcher: Your conscious mind can be an appreciative fan of the capacity of your unconscious mind to realize new levels of comfort.

Example Two:

Pitcher: What are you experiencing right now?
Receiver: I am curious about what you will do next.
Pitcher: There can be curious ways to focus inside.

Purpose: To define the utilization state. To practice utilization and tailoring. The Pitcher turns the Receiver's responses into hypnotic suggestions. To note how a small change in emphasis can lead to an alteration in response.

EXPERIENTIAL EMPOWERMENT
PSYCHOAEROBIC$_{SM}$ Exercises
www.psychoaerobic.org

PSYCHOAEROBIC EXERCISE 27

Clinician Posture to Develop: Communicate for strategic effect. Multilevel communication.

Format: Dyads.

Roles: One Pitcher; one Receiver.

Method: The Receiver closes his eyes. The Pitcher provides an induction of hypnosis. The Receiver is *not* informed of the method to be used. The handout can be given to the Receiver after the exercise, or the Receiver leaves the room and the exercise is explained to the Pitcher.

The sole method to be used is sets of recursive triplicates. A recursion is a theme presented with a modification; it is not a repetition. For example, "You are learning important things...things that really can stay with you...things that provide new meaning."

Use recursions for the four hypnotic goals: alter attention, modify intensity, dissociate, and build implicit responsiveness.

Discuss the state of being strategic.

Variation: Use the recursive processes to suggest a clinical goal, e.g., role-play a problem such as the inability to stop smoking or fear of flying. Use recursions for important interventions.

Purpose: Strengthen the message. Recursions provide an opportunity for the listener to better absorb conceptual messages.

EXPERIENTIAL EMPOWERMENT
PSYCHOAEROBIC$_{SM}$ Exercises
www.psychoaerobic.org

PSYCHOAEROBIC EXERCISE 28A

Clinician Posture to Develop: Strengthen the message. Be metaphoric.

Format: Dyads

Roles: One Pitcher; one Receiver.

Method:

Exercise 1: The Receiver role-plays a patient with a simple problem involving mild anxiety/depression, a habit, or a relationship issue. The Pitcher responds with simple phrases and uses hand and arm gestures—reflecting back empathic understanding of the Receiver's emotional message, e.g. "What you are experiencing is something like this (make gesture)." "Or, is it more like this (make another gesture)?" The Pitcher should think analogically. What is the expressed or underlying emotion? Whenever an emotion is expressed, the Pitcher communicates it back and enhances it with a symbolic gesture. The Pitcher should limit words and primarily use gestures. The words are the "scaffolding," the gestures are the foundation.

Continue the exercise for at least 10 interventions. Go slowly. Discuss the impact for each participant. What "state" was elicited? Remember, this exercise is designed to develop states in the Pitcher, not cure the patient.

Exercise 2: Reverse roles. The Pitcher responds to the Receiver's problem with sounds instead of gestures. Whenever an emotion is expressed, communicate it back using minimal words, and enhance it with a sound or a series of sounds. It can be a guttural sound, a syllable, a bar of music, a whistle, etc. Continue for at least 10 interventions. For example: "Is the feeling more "Whoosh" or "Whoosh!!?"

Purpose: To learn the use of gesture and sound. Gestures and sounds are signals. Signals elicit emotions, not words. Create living metaphors. Improve empathy by making it visual and auditory.

EXPERIENTIAL EMPOWERMENT
PSYCHOAEROBIC$_{SM}$ Exercises
www.psychoaerobic.org

PSYCHOAEROBIC EXERCISE 28B

Clinician Posture to Develop: Strengthen the message. Be metaphoric. Utilization.

Format: Dyads.

Roles: One Pitcher; one Receiver.

Method: This is a continuation of 28A. Return to original roles.

Exercise 3: The Receiver role-plays a patient with a simple problem involving anxiety, depression, a habit, or a relationship issue. The Pitcher responds with a simple phrase that introduces the use of an object to demonstrate empathetic understanding of the Receiver's emotional message, e.g. "What you are experiencing is something like this (using object)." "Or, is it more like this (using object differently)?" The Pitcher should think analogically, "What is the expressed or underlying emotion like?" Whenever an emotion is expressed, the Pitcher communicates it back and enhances it with a symbolic action with an object. The object can be anything at hand, a pencil, eyeglasses, or coffee cup. The object can be varied or the same object can be used repeatedly. The Pitcher should limit the number of words used. In this exercise they are secondary to the use of objects.

Continue for at least 10 interventions. Go slowly. Discuss the impact for each participant. What "state" was elicited? Remember, these exercises are designed to develop states in the Pitcher, not cure the patient.

Exercise 4: Reverse roles. The Pitcher responds to the Receiver's problem by asking about exceptions, e.g., "What is it like when you are doing better (or when you are happy)?" "What else is it like?" The Pitcher can use gestures, sounds, and/or objects to intensify the realization of exceptions. Solutions states have components. What are they? Learn to symbolize them and create living metaphors.

Variation: The Pitcher responds to the Receiver's communication by using postures.

Purpose: Strengthen the message. In Exercise 3, empathy is strengthened. In Exercise 4, solution-focused therapy is strengthened. Interventions in any therapy school can be strengthened experientially.

EXPERIENTIAL EMPOWERMENT
PSYCHOAEROBIC$_{SM}$ Exercises
www.psychoaerobic.org

PSYCHOAEROBIC EXERCISE 29

Strengthen the Message Drill

Ciinician Posture to Develop: Strengthening the message. Multilevel communication.

Format: Triads

Roles: One Pitcher; one Receiver; one Coach.

Method: The Receiver closes his eyes. The Pitcher conducts an induction to elicit relaxation. At regular intervals, the Coach suggests to the Pitcher any of the following variations:

1. Provide strategic pauses.
2. Strategically alter the tempo of speech.
3. Strategically alter posture.
4, Use prosody.
5. Use recursions (repetitions with slight variation).
6. se gesture for emphasis.
7. Strategically add sounds.
8. Strategically use proximity.
9. Increase the use of imagery.
10. Use metaphor.
11. Use linkage to make the communication one continuous sentence.
12. Use the SIFT process.

At the direction of the group leader, the Coach and Pitcher change roles.

Variation: Rather than an induction, role-play a problem.

Purpose: The Pitcher defines experientially what it is like to strengthen the communication.

PSYCHOAEROBIC EXERCISES 30-35:
An Introduction

The next series of exercises covers the domains (states) of tailoring, gift-wrapping, and psychological-level communication – additional concepts for strengthening messages. A brief orientation is provided because these are broad categories that cannot be comprehensively covered in this book:

Tailoring is a matter of speaking the recipient's experiential language. It requires assessing characteristics of that person to whom the message is directed, including linguistic components, interpersonal patterns, perceptual orientations, and significant personal history. To tailor, consider the client's values, patterns, and habits. Those who excel at tailoring quickly understand the position another takes in this world—a position that can be either positive or negative. For example, one person can value service, while another may be self-centered. One person can extol the positive, while another can be inclined to complain. Once a person's values and inclinations are understood, the message can be filtered through the person's lens. For instance, if a person values art, change can be oriented artistically. If a person constantly complains and wants to stop smoking, whenever he feels an urge to smoke, he can be directed to complain to someone. (Preferably, the complaint is about something other than smoking.)

The second concept, gift-wrapping (introduced in Psychoaerobic Exercise 1), is further addressed in the next set of exercises.

A third concept for strengthening a message is the use of psychological-level communication. Therapists understand that what a patient says and what a patient means may not coincide. Oftentimes, the therapist explains to the patient what he really means. Freud's dictum was, "Where id was, there ego shall be." However, if a patient is savvy enough to say one thing and mean another, the therapist should be equally savvy. Using multilevel communication activates patient realizations. It is another method of creating the dots so that the patient, to his or her own delight, can connect them.

All three of these domains are best understood and realized as concepts and states. Some didactic information can facilitate learning, but experiential methods will be more effective at creating concepts, states, and identities that can empower clinicians

EXPERIENTIAL EMPOWERMENT
PSYCHOAEROBIC$_{SM}$ Exercises
www.psychoaerobic.org

PSYCHOAEROBIC EXERCISE 30: CONDENSED SOUP I

Clinician Posture to Develop: Tailoring.

Format: Triads.

Roles: One Receiver; two Pitchers.

Method: The Receiver provides three positive self-descriptive adjectives, e.g., kind, cheerful, altruistic. The Receiver closes her eyes. The Pitchers conduct a double induction of hypnosis or progressive relaxation, each speaking consecutively.

The first Pitcher uses 20 words. One of the words must be one of the three self-descriptive adjectives provided by the Receiver. The second Pitcher continues the induction where the first Pitcher left off, and again must use one of the three self-descriptive adjectives. However, the second Pitcher has only 19 words left to use. The Pitchers continue the induction, each time using one less word, but including one of the self-descriptive adjectives. The exercise ends when one of the Pitchers says the final word, which must be one of the self-descriptive adjectives.

Note that the descriptive words can be modified, e.g., "beautiful" could be used as "beauty full." "Responsible" could become "response-able." Many words have multiple meanings, e.g., "open" can be used to express an attitude or an action.

The Receiver can provide feedback about the effect of tailoring, and can also experientially define what it is like to have a message tailored to his self-description. The Pitchers can experientially define what it is like to tailor a message to an individual. The Pitchers achieve the mentality of tailoring interventions.

Variations:

1. The Receiver provides three simple, personal goals, e.g., comfort, relaxation, and motivation, rather than self-descriptive adjectives. The Pitchers must address one goal each time they speak.
2. The Receiver provides two goals and two self-descriptive adjectives. The Pitchers must address either one goal or one self-descriptive adjective each time they speak.
3. The Receiver provides three adjectives that describe his prior experience of being in trance.

Purpose: To experience tailoring as a concept or state while keeping the goal in mind.

EXPERIENTIAL EMPOWERMENT
PSYCHOAEROBIC$_{SM}$ Exercises
www.psychoaerobic.org

PSYCHOAEROBIC EXERCISE 31: CONDENSED SOUP II

Clinician Posture to Develop: Gift-wrapping. Tailoring.

Format: Triads.

Roles: One Receiver; two Pitchers.

Method: The Receiver closes her eyes. Speaking consecutively, the Pitchers conduct a conversational double induction of hypnosis. This is a naturalistic method of hypnotherapy without formally defining the situation as trance. Their goal is to elicit relaxation. The Pitchers must work together to tell a coherent story. Before beginning the story, the Pitchers can huddle and agree on the content, theme, and characters in the story. Pitcher One begins by telling a story using only 20 words, perhaps counting on his fingers to keep track. To continue the goal of relaxation, Pitcher Two picks up where Pitcher One left off, and continues telling the story using 19 words. The Pitchers continue, each time using one less word. The exercise ends when one of the Pitchers says the final word.

Roles are changed. In the second iteration, the Receiver describes a personal interest and the Pitchers must directly or tangentially refer to the interest in each phase of telling the story. In the third iteration, the Receiver defines a simple personal goal (other than hypnotic relaxation) and the Pitchers consecutively tell the story to help effect that goal.

The Receiver experientially defines what it is like to receive a gift-wrapped message. The Pitchers can experientially define what it is like to gift-wrap (orient toward) within a story.

Purpose: Gift-wrap and keep the goal in mind. Tailor the message to the person's values, goals, and interests.

EXPERIENTIAL EMPOWERMENT
PSYCHOAEROBIC$_{SM}$ Exercises
www.psychoaerobic.org

PSYCHOAEROBIC EXERCISE 32

Clinician Posture to Develop: Tailoring. Attunement.

Format: Dyads.

Roles: One Pitcher; one Receiver.

Method: The Receiver keeps his eyes open. The Pitcher provides a short induction of hypnosis, using progressive relaxation, or active imagination. The Receiver is *not* informed of the method to be used. The Receiver leaves the room and the exercise is explained to the Pitcher.

The method to be used is decided by the Pitcher. There is a brief interview about hobbies and interests prior to beginning the exercise. Two short inductions are offered, one in which, from the outset, the Pitcher attunes to the Receiver's gestures and postures nonverbally by mirroring. The mirroring should be inconspicuous. It is helpful to mirror with a one-second delay and make approximations that are not obvious. For example, if the Receiver has his head tilted to one side, the Pitcher tilts her head just slightly but similarly.

Switch roles. The new Receiver leaves the room and the exercise is explained to the new Pitcher. There is a brief interview about hobbies and interests prior to beginning the exercise. Two short inductions are offered, one in which, from the outset, the Pitcher subtly attunes to the Receiver. The Pitcher uses mirroring in a refined way, speaking only when the Receiver exhales, coordinating his blink rate with the Receiver's, using the natural speaking tempo of the Receiver, mirroring the linguistic style of the Receiver, etc.

Discuss the state of implicit attunement.

Variation: Use the processes to suggest a clinical goal, e.g., stop smoking or be comfortable in an airplane.

Purpose: To implicitly attune to another person to increase responsiveness. To subtly build an alliance.

EXPERIENTIAL EMPOWERMENT
PSYCHOAEROBIC$_{SM}$ Exercises
www.psychoaerobic.org

PSYCHOAEROBIC EXERCISE 33

Clinician Posture to Develop: Gift-wrapping. Psychological-level communication.

Format: Triads.

Roles: Each person is a Pitcher in conversation with the other two participants.

Method: Throughout the exercise, all three participants pantomime holding and gently rocking a young child. In conversation with each other, each participant will describe in three or four sentences the furniture in a living room, but their communication must subtly imply something sexual. For example, in describing a table, one participant can talk about exploring the smoothness of the legs. The participants are to speak so that the "child" remains comfortable, does not recognize the implicit meaning of the description, and is not disturbed by the content.

The participants must compose a multilevel message and define experientially what it is like to compose and deliver it.

Purpose: To experience multilevel communication.

EXPERIENTIAL EMPOWERMENT
PSYCHOAEROBIC$_{SM}$ Exercises
www.psychoaerobic.org

PSYCHOAEROBIC EXERCISE 34

Clinician Posture to Develop: Gift-wrapping. Psychological-level communication.

Format: Triads.

Roles: Each participant engages in conversation, speaking three or four sentences in succession.

Method: The participants enter into a conversation and talk from the position of a child. They imagine an adult standing close by. They talk about toys, but the implied meaning of their communication is "keeping a secret." The object is to talk obliquely from a child's position so that the adult cannot understand the communication.

The participants must compose a multilevel message and define experientially what it is like to compose and deliver it.

Purpose: To experience multilevel communication.

EXPERIENTIAL EMPOWERMENT
PSYCHOAEROBIC$_{SM}$ Exercises
www.psychoaerobic.org

PSYCHOAEROBIC EXERCISE 35

Clinician Posture to Develop: Communicate on multiple levels.

Format: Triads.

Roles: One Pitcher; two Receivers.

Method: The Receivers leave the room while the Pitcher is instructed by the group leader. The Receivers return, and the Pitcher offers both Receivers the same hypnotic induction. The Pitcher talks simultaneously (as much as possible) to both the Receivers, suggesting comfort to one and arm levitation (or vivid memories) to the other.

Define experientially what it is like to speak on multiple levels. Change roles after the exercise.

Variations:

1. The Pitcher uses a slightly different voice tone when speaking to each Receiver.
2. The Pitcher paces the breathing rate of the Receiver being addressed, speaking only when that person exhales.
3. Each Receiver indicates one trance goal. The Pitcher tailors the induction to the goals of the Receivers.

Purpose: To experience multilevel communication.

PSYCHOAEROBIC EXERCISES 36-42:
An Introduction

The following six exercises are meant to develop utilization, one of the key states that define an Ericksonian orientation. Utilization is the foundation of solutions. (For more information, see the chapter on utilization in my book, *Confluence,* 2006.)

Utilization is a philosophy of sufficiency. It is the opposite of psychological problems, where there is an absence of utilization. Oftentimes in therapy, the patient believes that he does not have the resources to change or cope. In contradistinction, the therapist experientially demonstrates to the client that such resources exist. Something is present in the totality of the therapeutic/life situation that can be used constructively. All of Dr. Erickson's cases are based in utilization. It is the fulcrum that facilitates change.

Ponce de Leon did not find the Fountain of Youth in Florida, but Milton Erickson discovered a fountain of utilization in Phoenix. For therapists, utilization is an elixir, an antidote to burnout, the juice that keeps them vibrant and alive. Creativity is a byproduct of utilization.

Erickson's cases indicate how utilization is the progenitor of creativity. One famous case concerns a psychiatric patient who believed he was Jesus Christ and aggressively tried to convert hospital staff and other patients to Christianity. Dr. Erickson approached the patient and said, "Sir, I've heard you have experience as a carpenter." When the patient confirmed this, Dr. Erickson ushered him into the woodworking shop so that he might engage in more constructive activities. Dr. Erickson utilized the patient's metaphor.

Utilization is a state, not a technique. It is the first state to access when conducting therapy. It is the essential trance of the therapist. The therapist enters the utilization state and becomes "response ready," ready to respond constructively to any given situation.

To develop the state of utilization, the exercises that follow must be practiced repeatedly. Psychoaerobic Exercise 36 may be the most important exercise in this book, so practice it even more.

Note: A lecture on utilization, which includes a demonstration of Exercise 36, can be found on YouTube in the behavioral science video collection of California Southern University, where I am a Distinguished Professor. In addition, there also is a video of a discussion that I had with Richard Simon, the editor of the *Psychotherapy Networker,* about a demonstration induction Dr. Erickson conducted at a hypnosis conference in 1964. The video shows that the methods that Dr. Erickson uses arise from his utilization state, not from the application of techniques. (Links to both videos can be found at www.psychoaerobics.org.)

EXPERIENTIAL EMPOWERMENT
PSYCHOAEROBIC$_{SM}$ Exercises
www.psychoaerobic.org

PSYCHOAEROBIC EXERCISE 36

Clinician Posture to Develop: Utilization.

Format: Triads.

Roles: One Receiver; one Pitcher; one Coach.

Method: This exercise is for the Pitcher's development. The Receiver primarily serves as someone to whom the Pitcher can address. The Coach is an "irritant." As will be seen, both the Coach and the Receiver will help the Pitcher by providing feedback after the exercise.

The Receiver closes her eyes. She is instructed to protect herself and not be vulnerable. The Pitcher conducts an induction of hypnosis. A "utilization" induction is preferred, in which emitted behavior and environmental stimuli are reshaped in the direction of trance phenomenology—guide the attention, modify intensity, elicit dissociation, and build implicit responsiveness. (Alternatively, the Pitcher can offer relaxation training, guided imagery, or role-play any therapy protocol.) After approximately two minutes into the induction, the Coach, using the categories listed below, unexpectedly calls out words or provides sounds at 30-60 second intervals. The Coach provides eight intrusions, two in each category.

1. The Coach names different objects in the room—table, chair, window.
2. The Coach provides names of positive or negative internal states or emotions, e.g., comfort, curiosity, tension.
3. The Coach provides auditory stimuli, e.g., claps hands, snaps fingers, stamps feet.
4. The Coach offers random ideas, e.g., hamburger, football, South America.

The Coach uses two stimuli in each of the four categories, i.e., two objects, followed by two internal states, etc. There is an interval between each intrusion, so that the intrusion is unexpected. The Pitcher must immediately incorporate the Coach's concept into the induction patter, and then continue the established induction. After a short time, the Coach unexpectedly provides the next intrusion.

The Pitcher can utilize word plays, idioms, homonyms, and proverbs. For example, if there is a sound from a door, the Pitcher can reply, "You can open new doors of perception." If there is a sound of something dropping to the floor, the Pitcher can reply, "...and things can effortlessly drop into place." If the Coach calls out, "floor," the Pitcher can offer, "You can ground yourself in developing comfort." If the Coach calls out, "South America," the Picher can suggest, "You can explore over and over the borders of traveling down into developing areas of comfort."

During the course of the exercise, the Pitcher should achieve moments of accessing the utilization state. This state can be described as one would describe any other state, such as hypnosis, interest, or curiosity. Immediately after the exercise ends, the Pitcher describes his utilization state. Again, the States Table can be used.

After the exercise, the Receiver and Coach provide behavioral feedback (auditory and visual feedback respectively) as to how the Pitcher sounded, and what the Pitcher looked like when she seemed to best achieve the utilization state. This will allow the Pitcher to "anchor" those changes and enhance her utilization state. The Receiver does not talk about his trance experience. The focus is on helping the Pitcher achieve the state of utilization.

This is not an easy exercise to master, and often the Pitcher will be more "elephant" than elegant. But, Pitchers are given eight chances to realize the subjective sense of utilization. Realizing it momentarily is a start to developing the utilization state in procedural memory.

Switch roles and repeat the exercise so each gets a turn as Pitcher, Receiver, and Coach.

Purpose: To experientially define the "utilization state." Rather than conceptualizing utilization as a technique, it is best to realize utilization as an experiential posture or state.

EXPERIENTIAL EMPOWERMENT
PSYCHOAEROBICSM Exercises
www.psychoaerobic.org

PSYCHOAEROBIC EXERCISE 37

Clinician Posture to Develop: Utilization.

Format: Dyads. One Pitcher; one Receiver.

Method: The Pitcher conducts an induction using whatever methods she prefers. A utilization induction can use used. A utilization induction consists of feeding back emitted behavior in the direction of trance phenomenology (eliciting changes in attention, intensity, dissociation, and response).

After establishing the trance, at regular intervals (every few minutes), the Pitcher asks the Receiver to respond verbally to the question, "What are you experiencing right now?" or "What's happening right now?" The Pitcher takes whatever response the Receiver provides and either magnifies it if it is positive, minimizes it if it is negative, describes a reference experience for the phenomenon, or offers a common everyday example of it. There are differences between reference experiences and common everyday examples: Reference experiences are events in personal history; common examples are general. A reference experience could be introduced with the phrase, "You have had the personal experience of..." a common everyday example with the phrase, "We all have had the experience of..."

Example One (magnify):
Pitcher: What are you experiencing right now?
Receiver: Quiet.
Pitcher: You're *really* quiet inside...

Example Two (reference experience):

Pitcher: What are you experiencing right now?
Receiver: Quiet.
Pitcher: You've had the personal experiencing of enjoying quiet. For example, you can remember being at the beach on a warm summer day when you...

Example Three (common example):
Pitcher: What are you experiencing right now?
Receiver: Quiet.
Pitcher: A person can be driving in a car and not hear the sound of the engine. Experientially there can be internal quiet.

Example Four (minimize):
Pitcher: What are you experiencing right now?
Receiver: Tension.
Pitcher: There can be *a little bit* of tension at this moment *in some specific area*.

Purpose: To access three generic Ericksonian postures of utilization: amplify a deviation, access reference experiences, and utilize common everyday experiences. Clinicians can utilize social circumstances.

EXPERIENTIAL EMPOWERMENT
PSYCHOAEROBIC$_{SM}$ Exercises
www.psychoaerobic.org

PSYCHOAEROBIC EXERCISE 39

Clinician Posture to Develop: Utilization.
Format: Triads
Roles: Two Pitchers; one Receiver.

Method: This exercise is for the Pitcher's development. The Receiver primarily serves as someone to whom the Pitcher can address. The Receiver must self-protect and cannot be vulnerable.

The Pitchers conduct a simple induction to elicit trance. Pitcher One begins the induction and, after a while, makes an obvious "mistake," e.g., by coughing, blocking, or using "incorrect" form, e.g., using authoritarian rather than permissive verbs ("You will go deeper" rather than "You can go deeper"). Pitcher Two picks up where Pitcher One left off and must immediately respond by utilizing Pitcher One's mistakes.

Here are some examples: "Your unconscious mind can cough up many pleasant experiences that you can enjoy." "You can block out time for you to enjoy developing comfort." "Your inner mind can have its own will that can help you experience increasing comfort."

After utilizing the mistake, Pitcher Two continues the induction. Then, after a while, Pitcher Two makes an obvious mistake that Pitcher One must utilize to continue the induction. Each of the Pitchers will make and utilize five or six mistakes, after which the induction can be terminated. Then, roles can change, and the Receiver can become one of the Pitchers and one of the Pitchers becomes the Receiver until all have a turn being Pitcher and Receiver.

The Pitchers further define aspects of entering a utilization state.

Purpose: To define the utilization state. Even "mistakes" can be utilized.

EXPERIENTIAL EMPOWERMENT
PSYCHOAEROBIC$_{SM}$ Exercises
www.psychoaerobic.org

PSYCHOAEROBIC EXERCISE 40

Clinician Posture to Develop: Utilization.

Format: Dyads.

Roles: One Pitcher; one Receiver. Roles change from Condition One to Condition Two.

Method:

Condition One: Before breaking into dyads, the group leader asks participants to randomly call out three or four words. The Pitcher must conduct an induction of hypnosis by telling the Receiver a story that incorporates all of the words.

Condition Two: The group leader asks participants for the name of an object in the environment, the name of an article of clothing, a sound, and an emotion. The participants change roles and the new Pitcher conducts an induction of hypnosis by creating a story that incorporates all four words.

Variation: Rather than incorporating the words into a story, merely utilize them to create an induction.

Purpose: The Pitchers define and develop their utilization state.

EXPERIENTIAL EMPOWERMENT
PSYCHOAEROBIC$_{SM}$ Exercises
www.psychoaerobic.org

PSYCHOAEROBIC EXERCISE 41:

Tailoring and Reframing Drill

Clinician Posture to Develop: Utilization; Tailoring; Gift-wrapping.

Format: Dyads.

Roles: One Pitcher; one Receiver.

Method: The Receiver role-plays a simple, circumscribed bad habit, e.g., nail biting, procrastinating, or overeating. The Pitcher's goal is to "reframe" some aspect of the habit by gradually adding a positive connotation, by indicating some value it can have, and/or by finding positive intent behind the habit.

The class instructor selects words from the Receiver Characteristics list below, changing the words intermittently. When the Receiver is given a new characteristic, he must incorporate that characteristic into the role-play. The Pitcher must modify the reframe to fit the changing characteristics of the Receiver.

Change roles. The new Receiver role-plays a circumscribed problem. The group leader selects a gift-wrapping method from the list. The Pitcher must modify the reframe using whatever gift-wrapping technique the group leader calls out. The group leader changes the gift-wrapping randomly.

Note: Conduct this exercise slowly.

Receiver Characteristics:	Pitcher Technique:
(Tailoring):	(Gift-Wrapping):
1. Self-blaming	1. Anecdote
2. Withdrawing	2. Metaphor
3. Minimizing	3. Symptom prescription
4. Risk taking	4. Hypnosis
5. Exaggerating	5. Fantasy rehearsal

Purpose: The Pitchers experientially define what it is like modify the goal intervention by tailoring and gift-wrapping it.

EXPERIENTIAL EMPOWERMENT
PSYCHOAEROBIC$_{SM}$ Exercises
www.psychoaerobic.org

PSYCHOAEROBIC EXERCISE 42:

Echo and Strategically Modify

Clinician Posture to Develop: Strategic development. Utilization.

Format: Groups of five.

Roles: Four Pitchers; one Receiver.

Method: The Receiver is instructed to go into a trance during the exercise. The Receiver is to protect herself. It is not a time to be vulnerable.

Pitcher One leads in creating the induction, but can only say one or two sentences. Each subsequent Pitcher slightly modifies the first Pitchers' sentence(s) to elicit specific goals. Pitcher Two slightly modifies the sentence(s) of Pitcher One with the goal of having the Receiver slow down. Pitcher Three modifies the sentence(s) with the goal of having the Receiver intensify comfort. Pitcher Four modifies the sentence(s) with the goal of having the Receiver experience dissociation. Then, Pitcher One provides the next sentence(s), etc. The task is to modify the initial sentence(s) as little as possible and still elicit the goal.

Important: Each Pitcher should "live" the goal personally, prior to the presentation.

Here is an example:

Pitcher One: You can focus on the images you can see behind your eyes.
Pitcher Two: You...can...focus...on...the...images...you...can...see...behind... your eyes.
Pitcher Three: You can enjoy focusing comfortably and securely on the

images you can see behind your eyes.

Pitcher Four: You can consciously focus on the images you can see, while your unconscious mind can notice how they curiously change.

Discuss the states accessed by the Pitchers.

At the signal of the group leader, the Pitchers rotate roles so that each has a turn at providing the stimulus sentence(s) for modification.

Purpose: Offer the smallest modification that can elicit a systemic change.

PSYCHOAEROBIC EXERCISES 43-50:
An Introduction

The following exercises focus on therapist roles. Flexibility in social roles can be an asset to clinicians. It is easy to suggest this idea to students, but direct advice may not be helpful. Experiential practice of assuming flexible roles may be more effective. Moreover, the roles in the next section also can be considered states.

EXPERIENTIAL EMPOWERMENT
PSYCHOAEROBIC$_{SM}$ Exercises
www.psychoaerobic.org

PSYCHOAEROBIC EXERCISE 43

Clinician Posture to Develop: Visual acuity to detail (similar to Psychoaerobic Exercise 4); effect of changing therapist posture.

Format: Dyads.

Roles: One Pitcher; one Receiver.

Method: The Pitcher and Receiver sit face-to-face. The Receiver accesses an acuity state, looks at and "memorizes" the Pitcher. The Receiver closes his eyes, and then continues to access a state of acuity. The Pitcher makes three physical changes, e.g., readjusts clothing, takes off her watch, etc. The Pitcher orients the Receiver, who opens his eyes and identifies the changes the Pitcher made.

The Pitchers leave the room before Conditions One and Two, so that the group leader can provide instructions and perhaps a brief group induction. After both Conditions, the participants discuss the exercises and the effect of the group leader's instructions on both the Pitcher and the Receiver.

Condition One: The Receiver observes the Pitcher from the position of a critic. The group leader may offer a brief induction to assist the Receiver to access the role.

Condition Two: The Receiver observes the Pitcher from the position of a nurturer. The group leader may offer a brief induction to assist the Receiver to access the role.

Purpose: The Receiver must identify experientially what it is like to attend to visual details, i.e., describe the specifics of the "acuity state." The participants note the effect of changing the Pitcher's set.

EXPERIENTIAL EMPOWERMENT
PSYCHOAEROBIC$_{SM}$ Exercises
www.psychoaerobic.org

PSYCHOAEROBIC EXERCISE 44

Clinician Posture to Develop: Flexibility. Changing roles.

Format: Dyads.

Roles: One Pitcher; one Receiver.

Method: The Receiver closes his eyes. The Pitcher creates an induction of hypnosis to elicit relaxation. At the direction of the group leader, the Pitcher continues the induction, this time from the position of a salesperson selling the Receiver on the idea of relaxation. Alternatively, the Pitcher can take the position of a concerned parent, a spiritual advisor, a friend, a child, etc.

Purpose: To experientially define role changing.

EXPERIENTIAL EMPOWERMENT
PSYCHOAEROBIC$_{SM}$ Exercises
www.psychoaerobic.org

PSYCHOAEROBIC EXERCISE 45

Echo and Change Roles

Clinician Posture to Develop: Flexibility. Changing roles.

Format: Groups of six.

Roles: Five Pitchers; one Receiver.

Method: In order to help the Pitchers, the Receiver is asked to go into a trance and not be vulnerable. The Receiver then leaves the room while instructions are given to the Pitchers.

Pitcher One leads in creating the induction, but can only say one or two sentences. Each subsequent Pitcher repeats the sentence(s) that was offered by the first Pitcher, but can make modifications consistent with their respective roles: Pitcher Two accesses a state of curiosity, and presents the sentence(s) from that position. Pitcher Three repeats the sentence(s), having accessed a state of relaxation. Pitcher Four repeats the sentence(s), having accessed a state of enthusiasm. Pitcher Five repeats the sentence(s), having accessed a state of creativity.

Because the Receiver does not know each Pitcher's state, the Pitchers strive to ascertain the Receiver's response to each variation.

Variations:

1. After a few rounds staying within the proscribed roles, the Pitchers can select any of the four roles and deliver their interventions from that state.
2. The Pitcher can present the sentence(s) using other positive background states.

3. The Pitcher can use neutral and negative emotional backgrounds, such as being blasé, cautious disinterested, agitated, manipulative, etc.
4. The lead and four states: Curiosity, Relaxation, Excitement, and Creativity, are written on separate pieces of paper and put on the Pitchers' chairs. With each iteration of the lead sentence(s), the Pitchers rotate positions to communicate a different emotional background.
5. Rather than conducting an induction, role-play a simple problem. Whatever intervention Pitcher One makes, for examples, a question or a reflection is echoed by the next Pitchers from their respective roles. Go slow. The lead intervention from Pitcher One must be brief.

Purpose: The Pitchers learn how their "set" influences their communication. Also, the value of assuming roles flexibly.

EXPERIENTIAL EMPOWERMENT
PSYCHOAEROBIC$_{SM}$ Exercises
www.psychoaerobic.org

PSYCHOAEROBIC EXERCISE 46

Clinician Posture to Develop: Flexibility.

Format: Dyads.

Roles: Person A is the Therapist; Person B role-plays a Patient with a simple problem. Instructions are given privately to the Patient.

Method: The goal of the Patient is to make the Therapist happy by amusing and entertaining him/her. The Therapist naturally works to maintain "neutrality," thereby resisting the Patient's "induction." The interaction continues for 5-10 minutes.

Variations:
1. The Patient works to improve the Therapist's self-esteem.
2. The Patient tries to "induce" the Therapist into the Patient's own depression.

Purpose: The therapist maintains her own posture. Realize the power of social inductions.

EXPERIENTIAL EMPOWERMENT
PSYCHOAEROBIC$_{SM}$ Exercises
www.psychoaerobic.org

PSYCHOAEROBIC EXERCISE 47

Clinician Posture to Develop: To flexibly switch roles.

Format: Dyads.

Roles: One Pitcher; one Receiver.

Method:

The Pitcher communicates goals varying the presentation by assuming one of five roles:

1. The "fairy god person," who is nurturing, loving, and permissive.
2. The "police person," who is potent, protective, and rule bound.
3. The "engineer," or "technician," who is analytical and oriented toward facts.
4. The "rebel," who is spirited, tricky, and independent.
5. The "free spirit," who is playful, engaging, intuitive, and creative.

Recommendation: Access each role by first getting into a physical posture that represents the role.

The Pitcher offers a hypnotic induction (or a relaxation exercise) to the Receiver. At regular intervals, the group leader calls out for the Pitcher to use different roles (e.g., "intervene from the position of the fairy god person").

The Pitcher and Receiver change positions and repeat the exercise.

After terminating the exercise, discuss the interaction. Which roles were the easiest? The most difficult? Discuss the reciprocal induction of roles.

Variations:

1. The leader calls out for the Receiver to use different roles (e.g., "experience trance from the position of the rebel").
2. Role-play a therapist/patient interaction and make directed role changes.
3. The Pitcher secretly specifies a role, and then works to progressively inducc that role in the Receiver.
4. The Pitcher describes herself with an adjective and exaggeratedly intervenes from the state the adjective represents.
5. Prior to the exercise, participants are guided through an imagery exercise devised by the group leader to help develop five roles.
6. Gradually exaggerate each role as the Pitcher intervenes.

Purpose: To demonstrate flexibility. To establish "anchors" for different therapeutic roles.

EXPERIENTIAL EMPOWERMENT
PSYCHOAEROBIC$_{SM}$ Exercises
www.psychoaerobic.org

PSYCHOAEROBIC EXERCISE 48

Clinician Posture to Develop: To flexibly switch roles.

Format: Triads.

Roles: One Therapist; two Patients role-play a couple with a circumscribed problem.

Method:
As with Exercise 46, five roles are used:
1. The "fairy godperson," who is nurturing, loving, and permissive.
2. The "police person," who is potent, protective, and oriented toward rules and boundaries.
3. The "engineer," or "technician," who is analytical and oriented toward facts.
4. The "rebel," who is spirited, tricky, and independent.
5. The "free spirit," who is playful, engaging, and intuitive.

In an initial interview, the Therapist offers couples therapy. At regular intervals, the group leader calls out different role (e.g., "conduct therapy from the position of the fairy god person").

Discuss the interaction after terminating the session. Which roles were the easiest? The most difficult?

Change participant roles and repeat the exercise.

Variations:
1. When changing roles, participants can first assume a corresponding body posture for that role.
2. The Therapist describes herself with an adjective and exaggerat-

edly intervenes from the state that adjective represents.

3. Prior to the exercise, participants are guided through an imagery exercise devised by the group leader to help develop the five roles.

Purpose: To promote flexibility. To establish "anchors" for different therapeutic postures.

EXPERIENTIAL EMPOWERMENT
PSYCHOAEROBIC$_{SM}$ Exercises
www.psychoaerobic.org

PSYCHOAEROBIC EXERCISE 49

Clinician Posture to Develop: To flexibly switch roles.

Format: Dyads.

Roles: One person is the Pitcher; one is the Receiver.

Method: The Pitcher offers a relaxation induction (or guided imagery). The Receiver goes into a trance. The Pitcher changes roles at the request of the group leader and gradually and exaggeratedly induces trance components from the following roles:

1. Power
2. Voyeur
3. Loving
4. Martyr
5. Saint

Variations:

1. When switching roles, participants can first assume a corresponding body posture for that role.
2. Role-play a therapist/patient interaction and make directed role changes from the list.
3. The Pitcher secretly selects one of the roles, and during the induction works to progressively induce it in the Receiver. In the discussion period, discuss the reciprocal nature of roles.
4. The Pitcher chooses one role and gradually and exaggeratedly plays out that role.
5. Both the Pitcher and Receiver each secretly choose roles from the

list and gradually exaggerate those roles.

6. The Receiver role-plays a simple problem, and at the direction of the group leader, changes roles from the list above during the role-play.

Purpose: To access flexibility. To establish "anchors" for different therapeutic roles.

EXPERIENTIAL EMPOWERMENT
PSYCHOAEROBIC$_{SM}$ Exercises
www.psychoaerobic.org

PSYCHOAEROBIC EXERCISE 50

Clinician Posture to Develop: Flexibility.

Format: Groups of six.

Roles: One Receiver; five Pitchers.

Method: The five Pitchers are assigned one of the following roles: 1.) Goal-Setter, 2.) Gift-Wrapper, 3.) Tailor, 4.) Processor, and 5.) Role-Changer.

The Tailor briefly interviews the Receiver for assessment information. The Tailor asks five or six neutral questions, for example, about hobbies and interests.

The Pitchers work consecutively to induce a trance. The Goal-Setter announces the target suggestion, such as eye closure, deepening, arm levitation, hypnotic dreaming, and/or ego building, etc. Each Pitcher will modify the goal according to her defined role. The Gift-Wrapper choses a method to offer the goal, e.g., a metaphor or anecdote. The Tailor can then modify the method to fit the Receiver. The Processor can take the intervention and use the SIFT process. The Role-Changer can present the tailored and gift-wrapped goal from different states, e.g., curiosity, excitement, thoughtfulness, humor, etc.

Variation: At the direction of the group leader, participants change roles.

Purpose: The Pitchers learn to modify their methods and flexibly assume roles.

SUMMARY AND CONCLUSION

The Psychoaerobic Exercises present a number of domains that can be the foundation for a master Ericksonian therapist. Although these domains are derived from modeling Milton Erickson, they are clinician states that can empower any form of therapy. They include:

Being experiential
Developing acuity
Orienting toward
Being strategic
Strengthening the goal
Using multilevel communication
Being attuned
Creating constructive attributions
Effecting utilization
Tailoring
Gift-wrapping
Demonstrating flexibility in roles

These domains are most effective when learned experientially, rather than didactically. The process of training to develop specific sets is similar to athletes or actors developing their Ideal Performing State (IPS). Psychoaerobic Exercises have been developed for each domain. The intent is for therapists to develop the domains as concepts, states, and identities, so that they become procedural. The domains are vehicles for a therapist who wants to BE more excellent in therapeutic practice.

Science and art have evolved exponentially. In the 20th and 21st centuries, there has been a proliferation of scientific knowledge. Evolution in the arts has also been swift. For example, movies were invented in the early 1900s and conceptual developments have been rapid. Compared to today's standards, a movie produced 10 years ago seems amateurish.

Therapy has also evolved from its psychoanalytic infancy, but the evolution has been slow compared to the arts. There have been advancements in behaviorism, humanism, system approaches, cognitive-behavioral modalities, and affective neurobiology, however, therapy has primarily remained didactic. According to experts (Scott Miller, personal communication), in the last 40 years, effect sizes in meta-analysis of therapy have not improved. Therefore, it could be surmised that therapy has not substantially evolved. It is the thesis of this book that when the therapist evolves, so will therapy.

The therapeutic alliance is a significant factor that accounts for effect size, independent of therapist techniques and theories. To forge an alliance, clinicians can focus on experientially strengthening states within themselves.

This book offers a paradigm shift: The core of therapy can be conceptual. The goals of therapy can be conceptual. The supervision of trainees can be conceptual. A conceptual approach is not another school; it is an orientation that can be used in any approach.

Conceptual communication is easy to learn because we can rely on established artistic literacy. Conceptual communication can be used in all aspects of life when the goal involves eliciting an emotion, concept, or state. A methodology based on art has been offered for making it so.

Here are 10 "make its" for therapy that form the foundations of this book:

- Make it emotionally engaging.
- Make it visually interesting.
- Make it unusual to increase the impact.
- Make it precise.
- Make it in stages. Move in strategic steps.
- Make it dense. Strengthen the message
- Make it ambiguous to stimulate into play realizations that empower change. Use connotation. Orient toward.
- Make it conceptual.
- Make it in a way that elicits adaptive states.
- Make it experiential.

The conversation between therapist and client is unusual. It is uncommon when one person focuses so selflessly on another. To empower change, therapy has to be unique. Freud asked patients to lie on a couch and talk to the ceiling. His was an uncommon conversation. Freud was the first experiential therapist. We can further his vision.

An evolving person is a well-made instrument. Experiential training can be used to more effectively tune that instrument to optimize its range.

REFERENCES

Berne E. (1972). *What do you say after you say hello? The psychology of human destiny.* New York, NY: Grover Press.

Ekman P. (2006). *Telling lies: clues to deceit in the marketplace, politics, and marriage.* New York, NY: Norton.

Erickson, M. H., & Erickson, E. M. (2008a). The confusion technique in hypnosis. In E.L. Rossi, R. Erickson-Klein, & K.L. Rossi (Eds.), *The collected works of Milton H. Erickson, M.D.: Advanced approached to therapeutic hypnosis* (p. 5.), Vol. 4. Phoenix, AZ: The Milton H. Erickson Foundation Press.

Erickson, M. H., & Erickson, E. M. (2008b). Interspersal hypnotic technique for symptom correction and pain control. In E.L. Rossi, R. Erickson-Klein, & K.L. Rossi (Eds.), *The collected works of Milton H. Erickson, M.D.: Advanced approached to therapeutic hypnosis* (Vol. 4, p. 105). Phoenix, AZ: The Milton H. Erickson Foundation Press.

Gresham, W. L. (1946). *Nightmare alley.* New York, NY: Rinehart & Company.

Haley, J. (1973). *Uncommon therapy: The psychiatric techniques of Milton H. Erickson, M.D.* New York, NY: Norton.

Johnston, K. (1987). *Impro: Improvisation and the theatre.* New York, NY: Routledge.

Pines, A. M. (2002). A psychoanalytic-experiential approach to burnout. In *psychotherapy: theory, research, practice, training.* Washington, D.C.: American Psychological Association.

Spolin, V. (1963). *Improvisation for the theater: A handbook of teaching and directing techniques.* Evanston, IL: Northwestern University Press.

Sulloway, F. J. (1996). *Born to rebel: Birth order, family dynamics, and creative lives.* New York: Pantheon.

Zeig, J.K. (1980). *A teaching seminar with Milton H. Erickson.* New York, NY: Brunner Mazel.

Zeig, J.K. (1985). *Experiencing Erickson.* New York, NY: Brunner Mazel.

Zeig, J.K. (1987). The evolution of psychotherapy--fundamental issues. In J.K. Zeig (Ed.) In *The evolution of psychotherapy.* New York, NY: Brunner Mazel.

Zeig, J.K. (2006). *Confluence: The selected papers of Jeffrey K. Zeig* (Vol. 1). Phoenix, AZ: Zeig, Tucker & Theisen, Inc.

Zeig, J.K. (2014). *The induction of hypnosis: An Ericksonian elicitation approach.* Phoenix, AZ: The Milton H. Erickson Foundation Press.

ACKNOWLEDGEMENTS

There are many people whose help was instrumental in creating this book. I cannot adequately express the depth of my appreciation. Additionally, my thinking has been impacted by students who attended my workshops during the last 35 years.

The staff at the Milton H. Erickson Foundation work tirelessly to promote its mission. Our current staff includes Matthew Braman, Karen Haviley, Fred Huang, Christina Khin, Chandra Lakin, Chuck Lakin, Marnie McGann, Stacey Moore, Teresa Stratton, and Kayleigh Vaccaro, and. As director of marketing and publications, Chuck Lakin has been instrumental in the success of the Foundation.

Editorial assistance for this book has been provided by Marnie McGann, Suzi Tucker, Nicole Zeig, and Lori Deluca.

Members of the Erickson family have been staunch supporters of the Erickson Foundation. I am especially thankful to Kristina Erickson and Roxanna Erickson-Klein for their support over the years.